The Girl
I Never Knew

Who Killed Melissa Witt?

LaDonna Humphrey

Genius
Book Publishing

Milwaukee, Wisconsin USA

Published by:
Genius Book Publishing
4850 North 89th Street
Milwaukee, Wisconsin 53225 USA
https://GeniusBookPublishing.com

ISBN: 978-1-947521-81-0

220503 5x8

Table of Contents

This book is dedicated to Melissa Ann Witt

I didn't think it would end this way....

End? No, the journey doesn't end there. Death is just another path, one which we all must take. The gray curtain of this world rolls back, and all turns to silver glass. And then you see it.

What? See what?

White shores, and beyond, a far green country under a sunrise.

Well, that isn't so bad.

No, no it isn't.

—J.R.R. Tolkien

FOREWORD

Who shall tell the True Crime tale this week?

That is a question that is always on my mind. As a host and writer for True Crime Garage, a weekly podcast covering a new true crime case each week, the answer is almost always—me. However, that was not the case for the last week of November 2017. That week we would be releasing two episodes. I chose LaDonna Humphrey to tell the True Crime tale that week by describing to our listeners her passion for the unsolved murder of a girl I never knew. The case was that of Melissa Witt—a 19-year-old college student who was abducted on December 1st, 1994. It was unplanned, but the release date of our episodes would be less than a week before the 23-year anniversary of that nightmare.

There are so many twists and turns in the Melissa Witt case but one of the biggest surprises for me was the fire of this woman telling me about Melissa and the strange details surrounding her disappearance and murder. I was surprised because when LaDonna was just 15 minutes or so into our conversation, I asked, "And so you are someone who went to school with Melissa, or a family friend?" I was shocked to hear her say, "No, I never knew Melissa."

LaDonna and I spent hours on the phone that day. She told me every detail about the case and answered all of my questions, significant or otherwise. Her words were full of passion and intrigue. She spoke of Melissa not in a way that would suggest that she knew her; no, she spoke of Melissa in a way that told me that she cared for her. I left the conversation enlightened and with the knowledge that this forever 19-year-old Melissa Witt truly had an advocate. One of the best kind.

Along with my partner in crime who goes by the moniker "The Captain," we have been covering real life crime stories for years. During our time together on this dark journey we have encountered many, many tellers of true crime tales. Some, like us True Crime Garage boys, tell many different true crime tales. We cover just about everything under the sun. And because we cover a new case every week, just like anything else, it has its pros and cons. But we have also met many like LaDonna—people, that for one reason or another, have found themselves dragging along with them one tale. One story of hurt, loss and mystery that they have tasked themselves with spreading the word to any and all that will listen. Many do it for a multitude of reasons. Some because they've fallen in love with the mystery of their particular story. Some because they like telling the story and the reaction and response that comes with it. Some because they believe they may someday hold the solution that will unlock the mystery. I'm sure in some regard all of the reasons I have listed fall somewhere on the fringe of motives that drive LaDonna to carry Melissa's unsolved murder with her everywhere.

But what I know to be at the core of reasons for LaDonna are pretty simple and are as follows: One—LaDonna for some unique reason identifies with this forever 19-year-old Melissa Witt. Maybe she sees some of herself in Melissa. Or maybe if Melissa would have been allowed to grow up then perhaps the two would have become friends. Two—it is very important to LaDonna that Melissa is remembered always and even more so how she is remembered. Melissa was someone entirely so much more than a victim. She was really only a victim that one day of her short life, and victim is not a bad word. We don't choose to be victims, and Melissa certainly did not. She unfortunately became a victim by someone who lacks the ability to love. A person incapable of normal human thoughts and feelings victimized this young woman and has been hiding like a coward ever since. Three—LaDonna refuses to let Melissa Witt fade away. She has chosen the not so simple task of continuing Melissa's story. A story cut way too short against every fight and effort Melissa could muster. Some kind of monster with true evil in their heart got the best of that young woman on that night and none of us should ever be the same again.

This book is LaDonna's reminder to all of us that somewhere out there in the shadows evil lurks, and if this real-life nightmare happened to Melissa Witt, it can happen to any of us. That is why you and I stand up beside champions like LaDonna and say, "HELL NO!" Not one more girl. Not one more boy. Never again.

The first step to snuffing out evil is to recognize that it exists. That's the easy part. Next is to understand or attempt to understand evil. That is a dark journey that many cannot complete. Third is to seek evil out. Find it and confront it. My advice is to let your intellect guide you, not your heart. Last, when you find evil, hold its feet to the flames. The comfort only comes when it's all over.

LaDonna took up this fight. A fight for a girl she never knew. When that girl could no longer fight for herself, LaDonna was there and she will be in it neck deep until the end. That is her commitment. What is the end? See the previous paragraph. This book is one hell of a start.

LaDonna, like so many others, loves Melissa. She is still fighting for her tooth and nail. I am glad that she is, and I know that Melissa is as well.

—Nic Edwards
Host and Writer for the True Crime Garage Podcast

PREFACE

It seems strange to me to type out the words: I did not know Melissa Witt.

Technically, those words are true, I did not know Melissa in the traditional sense. I never saw her flash her dazzling smile. We never went shopping together. We never even had a conversation. I never knew Melissa Witt. And yet... our lives are deeply connected and forever intertwined.

How could that be possible? It's simple. I've spent seven years searching for the man who murdered her. I've spent countless hours poring over police case files, autopsy records, and crime scene photos. I've conducted hundreds of interviews, sent and received thousands of emails and Facebook messages, and stood in painful silence at the very spot where Melissa's lifeless body was discovered on a cold mountaintop in January of 1995.

I've sat in reverence as I've read the words that were penned by Melissa in her diary. As I write my own words in this diary of sorts, and openly share my heart about the Melissa Witt case in ways that I have never done before, my goal is that you, too, will come to know her. That you, the reader, will become so incensed with her murder that you, like me, will find it impossible not to seek and demand justice.

In an effort to be transparent and vulnerable, I have decided to write this story from my point of view, with only one goal: to find justice for a girl I never knew.

Chapter One
THE DISCOVERY

On January 13, 1995, the world, consumed by the murders of Nicole Brown Simpson and Ron Goldman, eagerly awaited the results of a hearing that would determine if evidence challenging Detective Mark Fuhrman's credibility would be admitted in the O.J. Simpson trial.

As I made my way along the winding roads leading to Fort Smith, Arkansas, I listened as the local radio station announced how prosecutors believed that O.J. dropped a glove as he attempted to sneak back to his mansion the night of the Simpson and Goldman murders. Judge Lance Ito was also expected to rule whether O.J. Simpson's former wife would be required to appear in court.

The unspeakable events surrounding the murders proved to be sensational, dark, and shocking. It was the perfect storm for a true crime addict. And I was hooked. At 21-years-old, I was already deep into my obsession. My fascination with murder mysteries gave me an adrenaline rush. The fix of the "who," "what," "when," and "where" kept me reading every true crime novel I could get my hands on.

On this particular day, as my obsession kept me tuned in to the radio for the O.J. Simpson case, another announcement caught my attention. A body had been found in the Ozark National Forest and authorities were on the scene. They suspected the body could be that of 19-year-old Melissa Witt.

As my Nissan Altima crept along the two-lane highway of U.S. 71 that was at the time the main route between Fayetteville and Fort Smith, Arkansas, I gazed into the Boston Mountains and watched dark clouds roll in.

At the same time, a chill settled in across the Ozarks. The clouds opened up and unleashed torrents of furious rain on a remote and lonely crime scene. As it turns out, roughly 56 miles away in the Ozark National Forest, a beautiful landscape of trees and mountains had been hiding a terrible secret.

On January 13, 1995 at 9:40am, about 15 miles north of Ozark, two animal trappers stumbled upon what they believed could be a mannequin lying face down in the woods about 30 feet off the main road. The two men, avid outdoorsmen, had walked this very path the day before. There had been nothing there.

As they approached the strange figure lying in the woods, it became clear that what they found was something much more sinister. After 45 long days, the remote Forest Service Road 1551 in the Ozark National Forest had finally unearthed the unthinkable: the decomposing nude body of a young, white female.

Frantic, the pair immediately called the Franklin County Sheriff's Department. Upon receiving the news, Sheriff Kenneth Ross contacted Detective Sergeant Chris Boyd with the Fort Smith Police Department Major Crimes Unit.

Over 20 years later, as I sat down to interview the now former Detective Boyd for a documentary I was producing on the Melissa Witt case, he could still vividly recall that cold and rainy morning.

"At the time, the police department was in the Sebastian County Courthouse and I distinctly recall walking through the basement to get to my office in the Detective Division. That's when I received a phone call from Sheriff Ross."

As the retired detective described the phone call, his expression turned serious and somber. I'd seen this look before. It was the expression of a man haunted by the unsolved murder of an innocent young woman.

"Sheriff Ross told me on that call that he thought he had found the body of Melissa Witt. And knowing him as I did at the time, I figured he was probably right. I had him describe to me what he was seeing and what the body looked like. Once he gave me the description... well, I knew I had to rally the troops at that point. We needed crime scene techs and detectives at that scene immediately."

As the former detective described the events that unfolded the morning of Friday, January 13, 1995, my own memories flooded back. When I close my eyes, I can still feel the icy chill in the air. I remember arriving in Fort Smith that morning, and as I stepped out of my car, the rain came down in heavy thuds, hard and fast, soaking my clothes as I ran across the parking lot. Another memory of me complaining to my coworkers about the miserable weather conditions on that day also replayed in my mind: "Why did this beautiful day take a drastic turn for the worst?" My words unknowingly foreshadowed events that would haunt me almost two decades later.

As the former lead detective on the Melissa Witt murder investigation, Jay C. Rider entered the room, I nervously stood to greet him. As we shook hands, Rider asked if Melissa and I had been friends, an assumption others often make to describe my passion for finding justice for a girl I never knew.

"No sir. I never knew her. We had mutual friends, but we never met." Rider eyed me skeptically, nodded, and said, "I guess that makes two of us."

"Tell me about January 13, 1995," I said. "The day you found Melissa Witt's body."

Rider described the day as normal, even for a Friday the 13th. "Don't get me wrong, I'm not a superstitious guy. It was a normal day. It started off sunny—a perfect day. I decided to get some work done around the office. When the phone call came in from Sheriff Ross, as you can imagine, all hell broke loose. We all headed out to that crime scene. We feared the worst… that this body was Melissa Witt."

News reports of the crime scene describe a lonely, remote logging road near Turner Bend just north of Ozark. I knew the location of Melissa's body would reveal details about her killer.

"Can you tell me more about the location?" I asked.

"It was a logging road. More or less a single lane road, rough terrain, off the main gravel area. The road was mainly accessed by loggers clearing and cutting the national forest," Rider explained. "Trappers, hunters, campers and sometimes local kids looking to party used that road. Believe it or not, the logging road ended—like a cul de sac—so it was a dead end. A remote, hopeless dead end."

"What else do you remember about that day?" I asked.

"I will never forget that day," Rider said. "We started working the crime scene and the temperature dropped drastically. It started to rain—hard rain—rain that was actually coming in sideways. The wind was blowing hard and it was miserable. None of us had jackets or anything else because it had started off as such a perfect day. I remember finding a raincoat in my car and trying to find a warmer shirt or something to change into so I could stay warm."

Rider's description of that fateful morning closely paralleled my own memories. But now it seemed that what we had witnessed was so much more than just a rainstorm. Instead, maybe we experienced the heavens releasing an unrelenting stream of tears for a girl we never knew.

The medical examiner's report revealed that the official cause of death was "asphyxiation by strangulation." Leaves and soil found in Melissa's airway indicated she had been strangled face down and she had inhaled debris from the forest floor as she fought for her life.

Laboratory testing on the debris found in Melissa's airway gave investigators an important clue: the debris was native to the Ozark National Forest. This told investigators that she had been killed at or near the location where her body was discovered. The medical examiner's report also yielded another important clue: Melissa had non-fatal trauma on the side of her head that was believed to have been caused by a blow or a fall.

Armed with this information, investigators began to put together a profile of Melissa Witt's killer. Two scenarios emerged: The killer was either a local or someone who frequented the area from out of state to hunt, hike, camp, or fish. Melissa's body could have been disposed of in many places but her killer chose this remote location. An area so isolated that if you had never been there before, it would be almost impossible to find.

A more detailed examination of the crime scene shocked investigators. Indentations behind a large headstone-like rock positioned between two small trees revealed that her body had initially been hidden there.

According to police records, Melissa had visible marks where someone, presumably the killer, had grabbed hold of her in order to drag her decomposing body closer to the road.

"It would have been a gruesome task," Jay C. Rider said flatly. "Think about it. Melissa's body had been out in the elements for 45 days and was in advanced stages of decomposition. There was small animal activity on the body and the scene was… it was brutal. Whoever moved that body did it so it could be found more easily. Maybe so her mama could give her a proper burial. Regardless, the task was gruesome and we are still trying to figure out who moved her body and why."

A strange phone call made to police a day or two prior to the discovery of Melissa's body may have provided a different clue. The caller left a voice message at the Fort Smith Major Crimes unit one evening. On the recording, a lady with a thick Southern accent could be heard saying, "Go ahead and tell them what you found." Then there was a younger male voice, also with a thick Southern accent who was reported saying, "No, I can't," and then the phone disconnected. Did the young man who was part of the mysterious phone call discover Melissa's body in the woods and move it from behind the rock so she could be found? Was he scared he could be blamed for the murder? Sadly, we may never know. Despite extensive efforts to identify the people responsible for that phone call, their identities remain a mystery.

Determined to learn more about the psychology of this type of killer and crime, I obsessively began to research homicidal strangulation. I discovered that in a high percentage of cases, the offender and the victim are related or in a romantic relationship. Seventy-five percent of strangulation victims are females, with the most frequent motives being rape, sexual jealousy, or personal rivalry. Research also suggests that females are predominantly the victims in homicidal strangulation because they are more likely to be the targets of sexual assaults.

Could this be why her body was found nude? Was she sexually assaulted? Unfortunately, we may never know for certain. According to the medical examiner's report, it was impossible to determine if she had been raped.

I kept researching. I found that a high percentage of female victims in homicidal strangulation are murdered due to a quarrel in their relationship and/or due to unrehearsed violence applied by bare hands to put the victim at a physical disadvantage and render the victim incapable of resisting. In 86% of the strangulation cases the victim was found at the scene of the killing. In 22% of these cases, the victim was found outdoors. In 17% of these cases, the offender stole something from the victim. In 14% of these cases, the victim was first hit with a blunt instrument.

A cold chill went down my spine. Did Melissa know her killer?

I compared these facts to what I had learned about her gruesome murder:

1) According to the autopsy report, Melissa was hit in the head with a blunt instrument.

2) She was found strangled, outdoors, and naked— her clothing and personal belongings had been taken from her.

3) The remote location was familiar to her killer. Authorities believe he had been there before.

I began to look even closer at events that had unfolded on the day Melissa disappeared. From all reports, the day started off routinely. She spent the first part of the morning with her mother, Mary Ann Witt. The honor student headed to Westark Community College next. After that, she went to lunch with a friend and then off to her job as a dental assistant.

Before she left that morning, Melissa had a minor disagreement with her mother. She had asked to borrow money, and Mary Ann, in an effort to teach her daughter money management, had told her no.

Before Mary Ann left for work that morning, she left a note for Melissa reminding her she would be bowling with her league that evening and offering to buy her a hamburger. She signed the note, "Love, Mom."

At five o'clock that night, after clocking out at her dental assistant job, Melissa discovered that her 1995 Mitsubishi Mirage wouldn't start. After a few tries, she gave up and waited with a coworker until a local businessman, later dubbed the Good Samaritan, gave her car a jump.

Police reports detail how Melissa's dome light was left on by mistake, draining the car battery. Investigators tracked down the Good Samaritan and interviewed him multiple times before ultimately clearing him in the teenager's disappearance and murder.

"People ask about the Good Samaritan all the time because those events leading up to Melissa's abduction seem suspicious," Rider said. "The Good Samaritan does seem suspicious, until you realize how many times he was questioned. He was cleared of any suspicion in Melissa's murder."

We know that, once Melissa's car started, she went home to change out of her uniform. Those clothes were found crumpled on her bedroom floor. Mary Ann was able to determine that her daughter had then donned a white V-neck sweater and blue jeans.

Melissa must have seen her mom's note, because authorities believe she headed to Bowling World, arriving between 6:30pm and 7:00pm. She parked in the northwest corner of the lot, but never made it inside. There were no cameras to record the events that unfolded in the parking lot that night. Witnesses would later tell police they heard a woman screaming, "Help me!"

Two decades later, as I pored over police files and news footage, my heart broke to learn that Mary Ann was haunted by the note she left for Melissa that fateful Thursday. In one interview she is quoted as saying, "I try not to think about how our lives would be different if I had not invited Melissa to Bowling World that night. There is no use thinking about it. I know she is gone. But my heart…. You know, as a mom… I sometimes wonder what if I had done something differently."

At approximately 7:45pm, Melissa's car keys were found in the parking lot and were turned in to the front desk of Bowling World. No one noticed the splatters of blood that were slowly drying on the metal keys.

Since Melissa never entered the bowling alley that night, her mother simply thought she had decided to go out with friends instead. Mary Ann went home expecting to see her daughter later that evening. Hours passed and Thursday slowly turned into Friday.

At nine o'clock on Friday morning, Mary Ann reported Melissa as a missing person. By Saturday, Melissa's friends and family were passing out flyers, blanketing the River Valley with over 6,000 pleas for help in finding the missing teenager.

I lived in Northwest Arkansas at the time, and remember seeing the story of Melissa's disappearance light up news channels. Her picture seemed to be everywhere. Curious, I reached out to my friends in the River Valley. It turns out they knew her. Their voices trembled as they shared their worst fears with me:

"Melissa would not just disappear like this."

"Where could she be? This is not like Melissa at all."

"I hope she's okay. I am scared she's been hurt."

Christmas passed and the new year rang in but there was still no Melissa Witt.

For more than a month, I, like the rest of the community, sat on the edge of my seat questioning what had happened to the beautiful All American Girl. None of us expected the story to turn into what it did.

A quote by the late Michelle McNamara, in her book *I'll be Gone in the Dark: One Woman's Obsessive Search for the Golden State Killer*, resonates with me. She wrote, "He loses his power when we know his face." These words sum up the rationale behind the countless hours I've spent investigating the Melissa Witt case. I want to see his face.

For over two decades the identity of Melissa's killer has been hidden among the dense trees and thorny undergrowth rooted deeply in the uneven ground of a remote mountaintop in the Ozark National Forest. I envision him, a shadow-like figure, dark and dreadful, his confidence anchored in the predictability of a murder case slowly growing cold.

Chapter Two
UNEVEN GROUND

In 2015, shortly after I began a journey to produce a documentary about Melissa Witt's murder, Jay C. Rider and Chris Boyd agreed to take my team to the site in the Ozark National Forest where Melissa Witt's body was discovered on January 13, 1995.

I was in no way prepared for the impact this would have on my life.

I vividly remember every minute of that day. The air was crisp and damp as we left Northwest Arkansas. My team was excited and looking forward to the filming schedule we had planned in the Ozark National Forest that afternoon.

We met the detectives at the Fort Smith Police Department. Once there, it was suggested that our team follow in our own car to see the "dump site" in Franklin County. The words "dump site" made me cringe and caused my stomach to lurch. I was overcome with a feeling of dread.

As we began to make our way to Franklin County, the words "dump site" replayed over and over in my head. I slowly opened the folder that was perched precariously in my lap. I shuffled through the contents until I found what I was looking for: the fresh-faced smiling photos of Melissa Witt. As I clutched her photo, I asked the rest of the team if they felt overwhelmed by the task ahead.

I only partially heard their answers.

"Yes. This drive is impossibly long," someone remarked.

"I don't see how he could have possibly kept Melissa subdued for this entire car ride," someone else said.

I vaguely remember nodding my head halfway in agreement with both their statements

"Dump site." Those words kept replaying.

It was too much for me to process. What a horrific and tragic end to such a beautiful life.

We sat in silence for the next half hour. There were no words worth exchanging. The mood had shifted drastically. The realization of what Melissa must have felt and endured during that car ride to the Ozark National Forest hung heavy in the air.

Despite the shining sun and our armed escorts, once we turned onto that remote logging road, I distinctly remember feeling panic. Can you imagine what Melissa must have felt? After an hour-long drive under the cover of night, she could have only felt sheer terror and helplessness.

"He never planned to let her go," I said.

As we pulled up, I turned to Connor, our driver, and added flatly, "He chose this spot to kill her."

Connor turned off the ignition and we slowly stepped out of the car. Detective Rider looked me squarely in the eyes and said, "If you screamed right now, nobody would be able to hear you." I took a deep breath. I knew he was right. There was nothing on this remote logging road except for dense trees, brush, and rough terrain.

"Nobody to hear you scream."

"Dump site."

Melissa's smiling photos.

"He brought her here to kill her."

As these thoughts closed in, I wanted to run, but like Melissa on that cold December night, I had nowhere to go. I was trapped.

As my camera crew began to unpack their gear, Detective Rider motioned for me to follow him. My steps felt heavy. He pointed to a large rock that loomed ahead on a small incline.

"Is that it?" I asked.

He nodded.

I walked ahead. Alone. I remember watching my steps. My thoughts were tainted with apprehension and despair. I was surprised at how rough the terrain was to navigate. I observed that the rock was on enough of an incline that it would have caused someone to struggle to reach it in the dark. It became apparent to me that this exact location was no accident. Melissa's killer had been here before. This location meant something to him.

My jumbled thoughts halted as soon as I realized I was standing right in front of that rock—the very place where 19-year-old Melissa faced down the monster that killed her.

I stood silently, trying to contain the sobs that I feared would overtake me. At some point, I could sense that the detectives were standing next to me. Once I acknowledged their presence, they began to take turns discussing the details of the crime scene. Their faces were somber. They spoke in hushed tones.

Detective Boyd reminded me of the autopsy findings— how those revealed that Melissa Witt had been strangled at that exact location.

"Are you sure?" I asked.

"We're sure," he said as he pointed to the place where Melissa Witt's life was stolen.

I had to look away... but I could not walk away.

My life was forever changed that afternoon as I stood on that uneven ground, in the very spot where Melissa Witt fought for her life. I vowed to begin my own fight that afternoon. A fight for justice for a girl I never knew. I was in no way prepared for the ways this vow would change and shape my life.

Coming to understand the horrific details of how Melissa died has been painful. Those final moments of Melissa's life were filled with panic, hopelessness, and terror. The massive amount of adrenaline pumping through Melissa's body released a powerful biochemical response of fear. This survival mechanism flooded every cell of her body, increasing her heart rate and fueling one last frantic attempt to save her life.

As her killer gripped her neck, the tightness around Melissa's throat sent signals to her brain alerting the panic centers to begin responding at a rapid pace. The fear center of her brain kicked into high gear causing her to instinctively thrash around violently in an attempt to fight off her attacker so she could breathe.

Inevitably, the damage to her larynx, the fracture of her hyoid bone, and the lack of oxygen to her brain would cause the once vibrant 19-year-old Melissa Witt to slowly fade into the black abyss of death.

Over the years the darkness surrounding Melissa's tragic murder has taken hold of me, giving birth to a recurring and frightening dream. Something or someone awakens me from a deep sleep. I walk across my house and open the front door. I am instantly standing in a densely populated forest. The forest is enveloped in a thick fog and it is difficult to see. Overcome with fear, I turn to go back into the house—but the house is gone. I am left standing alone in the forest.

Confused, I gaze at my feet and discover that I am barefoot. As hot tears stream down my face, a figure in white appears in the distance. The mysterious shadow motions me toward them. I shiver from the cold before cautiously moving in that direction.

Suddenly they become frenetic and signal for me to hurry. I run. Pain shoots through my feet as I make my way across the rough terrain of the frozen forest floor.

Despite the pain, I run faster. The cold air burns my lungs and my legs ache. The figure stops abruptly to remove the white, heavy veil masking their identity. Long blonde hair spills out, cascading down petite shoulders. I gasp as she points into the shadowy chasm of the forest. My heart races. Instinctively, I know she is pointing at the tombstone-like rock.

Without hesitating I scramble across the slight incline to get a closer look. I find that the forest floor is covered in a thick blanket of papers. As I hurriedly collect them, I notice that each one has one man's name written in bold, dark ink. My eyes strain to decipher the letters on the page, but the dark and murky forest makes this task impossible.

The haunting silence of the forest is shattered when a twig snaps behind me. I slowly turn to see a man standing just feet away. It's his name that is scrawled across the papers I am clutching. I am certain it is the man who murdered Melissa Witt. He takes a step toward me, his hands probing for me in the darkness. As he begins to speak, I scream then jolt awake.

Even in my dreams his face is concealed.

※

The combination of my disturbing dream and my vow to find justice prompted me to call Jay C. Rider and ask to meet again. I had more questions about the case. Questions only he could answer.

We sat down at a table inside an Olive Garden restaurant in Fort Smith, Arkansas. He eyed me suspiciously as

I opened a worn and tattered spiral-bound notebook. He pointed as he said, "I see you've come loaded for bear."

I shrugged, "It's just a few questions." I was reluctant to admit my notes actually spanned over two dozen pages.

After the waitress took our orders, I asked the now retired detective to help me understand why it took several days for the Fort Smith Major Crimes Unit to get involved in the search for Melissa.

Rider took a sip of water and said, "As the patrolman took the missing person report on the morning of Friday, December 2nd, one of the very first things he asked Mary Ann Witt was if she and Melissa had argued. Mary Ann told him there had been a brief discussion—a small dispute—when Melissa asked to borrow some money. Once he knew about the argument, well he chalked it up to a routine missing person situation. Melissa was considered an adult and it wasn't illegal for her to decide not to come home."

The patrolman was right. Melissa, age 19, was considered an adult and, in the United States, it is not illegal for an adult to "go missing." In fact, statistics show that over 600,000 people (ranging from young children to adults) go missing each year in the United States. The vast majority of those cases are resolved relatively quickly.

The report that was taken that morning was filed long before NCMEC (the National Center for Missing and Exploited Children) extended their services to cases of critically missing young adults aged 18, 19, and 20. (A critically missing young adult is one who is at an elevated risk of danger if not located as soon as possible, due to the circumstances surrounding their disappearance.)

When the missing person report was filed, little was known about the events leading to her disappearance. The patrolman only knew that a 19-year-old girl didn't come home after an argument with her mother. At that point, there was no evidence suggesting that Melissa had been abducted. The patrolman had assured Mary Ann Witt he had seen this scenario play out hundreds of times before. He was certain that Melissa would be home soon.

Rider continued, "We finally got boots on the ground to search for Melissa the same day news stations began airing footage of the concerns of possible foul play in her disappearance. Her friends and family had organized a massive search effort. After that aired, we received a phone call from a Bowling World employee who reported that on Thursday evening, December 1st, a set of keys had been turned in around 7:45pm."

That call from the bowling alley employee turned the Witt case upside down. The keys that were turned in by a construction worker and his family held an important clue. The name spelled out on the keychain was "Missy."

Three days after the initial report of the teenage girl affectionately called "Missy" by her friends and family was marked as a "runaway case," the tide shifted and the Fort Smith Police Department Major Crimes Unit began actively searching for the missing girl.

"How soon did you find Melissa's car?" I asked.

"Immediately," said Rider. "Because Mary Ann never saw Melissa at Bowling World that night, she never thought to search that bowling alley parking lot for her car. As investigators, that's the first place we looked. Once we found the car, we also found a gold hoop earring, a crushed hair clip, and pools of blood—all belonging to Melissa."

These clues pointed to something much more sinister than a runaway teenager. The race to find Melissa Witt was now in full swing. Every second mattered. Investigators knew that the first 48 hours was a critical window in a missing persons investigation. They were now well beyond that window of time.

Determined not to leave any stone unturned, detectives investigated Melissa's last known whereabouts: Bowling World. Investigators were stunned to learn there was no surveillance footage of the parking lot. Additionally, Bowling World only employed private security for weekends and on alternate weekdays. As fate would have it, there was no security present on Thursday, December 1, 1994.

Three years later, in February 1997, Melissa's family, the Parnells, would file suit against Bowling World. In Parnell v. C N Bowl Corp, her family alleged that the "defendant failed to exercise ordinary care to provide for the safety of business" in the following areas:

1) That the parking lot facility did not provide adequate lighting to allow a lone female to exit her vehicle and enter the premises operated by the Defendant safely and there were no warnings to

individuals that previous criminal activities had taken place on the parking lot facility and that they should take precautions in protecting their person and/or property;

2) By failing to warn the deceased that the parking facility was an area where known criminal activity had taken place frequently over the past several months before the abduction of Melissa Ann Witt, the parking lot facility maintained at the Defendant's place of business was unsafe for unaccompanied females to exit their vehicles after dark;

3) By failing to have security available at the parking facility on the night that the deceased was abducted and subsequently murdered;

4) By improperly utilizing security since security was only in place on two to three nights per week at the Defendant's parking facility and not available on days of the week known to the Defendant on which criminal activity had taken place on their parking facility in the past.

The Court concluded that the "tragic event which befell plaintiff's decedent was not foreseeable" and dismissed the case.

Twenty years later, Bowling World declined via email to participate in my documentary on the Witt case. The words "We would not be interested in filming on our property. Thank you." would be the only written acknowledgement of my request. As I have investigated the case, I shockingly discovered that Bowling World was not alone in their refusal to cooperate with my efforts. Others, however, like Jay C. Rider, enthusiastically participate in any effort to find justice for Melissa Witt.

As we sat together that evening in Olive Garden, the retired detective with the tough exterior said something unexpected: "I appreciate the time and effort you are putting into Melissa's case. Thank you for your passionate pursuit of the one thing I have always wanted in this case: the truth. Thank you!"

I sat in stunned silence for several minutes before thanking Jay C. Rider for his kind words. "It's an absolute honor to sit here with you today, sir, and to work on this case," I said humbly, meaning every word.

Neither Rider nor I could predict that six years after our meeting at Olive Garden, headlines from THV11 in Arkansas would read: "A retired detective and an Arkansas woman are working to solve Melissa Witt's murder." The reporter, focused on our mutual passion to find Witt's killer, also noted that "Rider and Humphrey have gained a friendship over their dedication to Melissa's case."

The ripple effects from my vow to find justice have sparked more than just friendship. People from all across the United States have sought my help in seeking justice for their loved ones. One such request came from a Missouri family. In a letter requesting assistance, the family provided a document cataloging the similarities between their daughter's case and the murder of Melissa

Witt. Intrigued, I combed the United States for other cases resembling Melissa's abduction and murder.

I stumbled across the case of Alana "Laney" Gwinner. Laney Gwinner, 23, disappeared from Gilmore Bowling Lanes in Fairfield, Ohio just after 12:30am on Wednesday, December 10, 1997. Earlier that day Laney had passed a college exam that guaranteed her an associate degree in business. She had so much to look forward to in life.

At approximately 12:35am Laney had telephoned her boyfriend, who lived less than two miles from Gilmore Bowling Lanes, to say she was leaving the bowling alley and would be at his house in a few minutes. She never arrived.

Laney, like Melissa, disappeared from the parking lot of a bowling alley on a cold December night. No witnesses. No security cameras. Nothing. The only difference: Laney's black Honda Del Sol, license tag AKP-3607, has never been located.

Thirty-one days later, on January 11, 1998, Covington, Kentucky Police Officer Mike Partin was in foot pursuit of a man wanted for minor offenses. As they crossed the Clay Wade Bailey Bridge over the Ohio River, Partin fell ninety feet to his death. During the search for his body, a deckhand on a tugboat noticed something floating in the river near Warsaw, Kentucky. It turned out to be the body of Laney Gwinner discovered nearly 60 miles from where she disappeared.

The coroner could not say if Laney's death was caused by suffocation or strangulation, only that she was dead before she was placed in the river. Investigators believe that Gwinner was accosted in the bowling alley's parking lot after rejecting the advances of her killer.

The disturbing similarities between the Witt and Gwinner cases compelled me to contact Ohio authorities. As I awaited their response, I kept digging through cold cases. The attempted abduction of Elizabeth Davey immediately caught my eye. According to news reports, on the evening of October 16, 2010, 24-year-old Elizabeth Davey was enjoying an evening out at the Blackiston Bowling Alley in Clarksville, Indiana.

Reports on the crime state that Davey first saw her attacker as he held the door open for her as she left the bowling alley—seconds before the attempted abduction began.

The would-be-abductor, Peter Allen Roberts Sr., placed a noose tightly around her neck as he forced Davey onto the floorboard of his truck. Roberts then proceeded to hold a knife to Davey's throat as he wrestled to keep her in the truck. Frightened for her life, Davey pleaded with Roberts to let her live, and she told him about her then one-year-old son. The brutal attack came to a stop when two men heard Davey's screams, opened the passenger-side door of the truck, and pulled Roberts away from Davey. At trial, Peter Allen Roberts Sr. was found guilty on all counts stemming from the 2010 attempted abduction of Elizabeth Davey.

I was overpowered by a haunting sense of deja vu as I read through details of the crime committed against

Elizabeth Davey. Could the Witt, Gwinner, and Davey cases be related? I needed to find out.

In an effort to learn more, I shared information about the Davey case on social media. I included a news article about Peter Allen Roberts, Sr., and his conviction in the attempted abduction of Elizabeth Davey. The social media post quickly gained momentum, and a myriad of armchair detectives filled my Facebook inbox with dozens of messages. Several of those messages described the distance between the two towns as a 126-mile journey that could be made in as little as two hours. The last message in my inbox, however, stopped me in my tracks. The author was Peter Allen Roberts, Sr. The message sent: "Hello."

Since that first correspondence, Roberts has sent me a dozen or more cryptic and disturbing messages. In response, I have replied to Roberts with a variety of direct questions related to the Witt, Davey, and Gwinner cases. To date, Roberts has yet to acknowledge any of my requests. Instead, he seems to prefer his own strange version of cat and mouse.

Despite the frustrating dead ends, I refuse to give up. Resolved in my commitment to find justice, I began sorting through the dozens of spiral bound notebooks stacked on my desk—each one brimming with handwritten notes about the Witt case. As I flipped through their worn pages, heavy with ink, I came across a familiar name. This man had called me dozens of times. As I read through my notes and reflected back on our late night phone calls, it was now apparent this man had been lying to me. Alarmed, I called Jay C. Rider.

Rider answered on the second ring. Unable to hold back, I blurted out the man's name and the nature of his phone calls. Stunned, Rider asked, "How long has he been calling you? I need to know everything he's told you. Start from the beginning. Go slowly. This is important."

And just like that, the decades old murder case exploded with new potential.

Chapter Three
DETECTIVE RIDER

When I met Jay Carl Rider in 2015, he was not what I expected. The physically fit then 65-year-old emanated a demeanor of intimidation and skepticism. His very presence commanded respect. Rider's rugged face and chiseled features were the perfect match for his tougher-than-nails personality. Rider's eyes, while kind, still reflected the dark memories of the horrific crimes he had witnessed over the span of his career in law enforcement. Years after our first meeting, when I sat down to interview him again, he described some of the crimes that still haunt his waking thoughts: "I've seen babies murdered, people beheaded, women mutilated, you name it. You can't shake it. It sticks with you… forever."

At our first meeting, the impeccably dressed Rider remained focused and serious. That posture would eventually change as we worked together on the Melissa Witt case. Rider's brash jokes and witty sense of humor are now a staple of our friendship. His laughter, genuine and contagious, is a welcoming distraction, as we dredge through the details surrounding the horrific murder of a 19-year-old girl.

I was only two years old in 1975 when Rider began his career in law enforcement as a patrolman with the Fort Smith Police Department. As he worked his way up the ranks, eventually retiring as Captain of the Major Crimes Unit, I grew, graduated high school, and delved into studying journalism at the University of Arkansas, while starting a family. I'm still in awe that our paths crossed. The vast differences in our ages, geography, and career choices all but guaranteed we would never meet. And yet, remarkably, an invisible string connected us to Melissa Witt's case.

When Rider and I first met, he was employed as an ABC (Alcoholic Beverage Control Division) Enforcement agent. Now retired from that position, Rider spends most of his time with his sweetheart, Marlena. Each week, like clockwork, the pair volunteer at an animal shelter. Rider also tends to his own beloved pets, his yard, and stays actively involved in the lives of his friends and family. The former Captain of the Major Crimes Unit has gracefully settled into a well-deserved life of routine normalcy.

Unfortunately, his life has not always been quite that simple. Back in 2005, Rider gained notoriety when the Federal Bureau of Investigation leveled serious accusations against him. The FBI alleged that Rider was part of an "inner group" in the Fort Smith Police Department. It was alleged they operated secretly, brandishing their own version of justice throughout the River Valley. According to news reports, eleven armed FBI agents swarmed Rider's home in connection with their investigation.

Eventually a grand jury was convened by the Public Corruption Section of the Department of Justice in Washington, DC. To my knowledge, no findings have ever been published in conjunction with their investigation. According to what I saw in news reports, the federal investigation seemed more akin to a witch hunt with those closest to the investigation claiming that intimidation tactics were used to frighten and harass would-be witnesses.

As you can imagine, the ordeal took a toll on Rider and his family, the weight of the unfounded accusations revealed in the sound of his cracking voice whenever he recounts the series of events that inflicted a lasting scar on his life.

Undeterred by the scandal, however, Rider bravely continued to protect and serve the River Valley and the surrounding communities. He also never gave up on his pursuit to find justice for Melissa Witt. Rider's valiant efforts to solve her case were beautifully memorialized in a letter written to him by Melissa's mother, the now late Mary Ann Witt:

> Captain Rider, I don't even begin to know how to thank you for all the time and effort you have put into Melissa's case. I can never repay you, but I want you to

know I appreciate your kindness, patience and consideration to me over the years. In spite of the fact that you have so many other responsibilities, you still find time to chase down leads you feel are a wild goose chase just because I ask you to. I want you to know I do not take that for granted. Also, please pass on my thanks to all the other officers who have worked on her case. Steve Howard. Lanny Reese. And others whose names I do not know. I appreciate every one of you. And someday, I hope we will all know who killed Melissa. If we do, I am sure it will be due to your efforts. Thank you and God bless you!

—Mary Ann Witt

The hardened detective, visibly touched by these words, shared details of his relationship with the grieving mother: "Mary Ann and I developed a really close relationship. She asked me at the very beginning to keep her apprised of all leads and I did my very best to do that. If I got a lead, no matter how bad it was, I always shared it with her."

Rider went on to describe his hopes of solving Melissa's murder in Mary Ann's lifetime: "I really wanted to solve this case. Mary Ann was desperate for answers. But I am going to keep working on this case until my own dying breath to get this case solved for Melissa and for Mary Ann."

Sadly, Mary Ann did not live to see her daughter's killer brought to justice. On Sunday, March 20, 2011, Mary Ann Witt passed away. She was 75. The loving mother was laid to rest next to her beloved daughter Melissa at Woodlawn Memorial Park in Fort Smith, Arkansas.

Rider often reflects back on the hundreds of people he encountered while trailing Melissa's killer. "We interviewed over 300 people. Sex offenders. Transients. The boy next door. You name it. We were determined, we still are determined, to find him," Rider said.

One of the men interviewed by law enforcement was Larry Landrum. Landrum, labeled a habitual criminal, was arrested on the afternoon of December 12, 1994 on an unrelated series of crimes involving the attempted rape and aggravated assault of a woman named Kristie Anderson and the theft of her property. He was taken to jail and scheduled to be arraigned on these charges on December 14.

"If my memory serves me well," said Rider, "we questioned Landrum on the afternoon of December 13th about Melissa Witt. We talked to him for about thirty minutes. He was also questioned about the Lucille Hassler murder case."

During questioning, Landrum's body language set off red flags for investigators, Landrum was asked if he wanted to take a polygraph examination and he agreed. The results of the polygraph indicated deception, and when confronted, Landrum eventually admitted that he had killed Lucille Hassler.

"Landrum was a bad guy," said Rider. "He was eventually convicted of Hassler's murder and sentenced to life in prison. We never did find any evidence connecting him to Melissa Witt's abduction and murder."

It turns out that Larry Landrum wasn't the only "bad guy" that Rider and his team questioned. William Dillard Taylor was also questioned about Melissa's abduction and murder. According to Rider, "Taylor was wanted in Arkansas on rape charges. He ended up stealing a gun from his sister's house and we had over two dozen officers looking for this guy."

At the time, Taylor was wanted in both Sebastian and Crawford counties in Arkansas. He was charged with raping a young girl in Sebastian county, and with rape and sexual abuse in Crawford county.

Eventually Taylor was caught and brought in for questioning. "We attempted to question Taylor about both the murder of Melissa Witt and the abduction of little Morgan Nick from Alma, Arkansas," said Rider. "We never connected him to either case, but we did look at him closely."

Interested in learning more, I decided to examine court records pertaining to William Dillard Taylor. The results were interesting. I discovered that Taylor had filed a pre-trial motion seeking a change of venue after he was captured and brought to trial on the rape charges. Taylor attached several newspaper articles regarding the case as exhibits to his motion. Taylor claimed that due to the pre-trial publicity, he could not receive a fair trial in either Sebastian or Crawford county.

The Court held a hearing on the motion to change venues. Taylor introduced the testimony of a man named

Marvin Honecutt, an attorney from Van Buren, Arkansas. Honecutt testified that he had seen extensive television and newspaper coverage about Taylor. According to Honecutt, most of the coverage he had seen was in regard to police efforts to question Taylor about the disappearance of a six-year-old girl named Morgan Nick and the murder of Melissa Witt. He was of the opinion that no juror in either county could give Taylor a fair trial because they would always have Melissa's murder and the abduction of Morgan Nick in the back of their minds. Taylor's motion seeking a new venue was ultimately denied by the Court.

Taylor's concerns about the pre-trial publicity in regard to the Witt murder sparked my curiosity. Did it really matter that the news reported Taylor was wanted for questioning? It seemed logical to me that authorities would want to talk to him. After all, he was considered to be a violent sexual predator on the run from law enforcement. Several of the news outlets also reported Taylor's three felony rape warrants involving children between the ages of six and fourteen. Why didn't Taylor find the allegations of child rape much more egregious than simply being wanted for questioning by authorities? I needed answers and decided to go directly to the source. I wrote a letter to William Dillard Taylor.

William Dillard Taylor, also known as Inmate #070160, is being held in the Arkansas Department of Corrections Cummins Unit in Grady, Arkansas. Taylor, convicted of rape, is serving life in prison. According to court records, Taylor's own daughter testified against him.

She alleged that when she was four-years-old, Taylor began molesting her. She also testified that eventually Taylor began raping her and the abuse sometimes involved her siblings and other men. He threatened to kill her mother and her sisters if she told anyone what was happening to her. Taylor's other children and stepchildren also testified that they were either molested or raped.

In my letter to Taylor I decided not to mention the months I'd spent reading court documents, news articles, and police records pertaining to the crimes he committed. Instead, I wrote to Taylor and introduced myself as an investigative journalist working on a documentary about the 1994 murder of Melissa Ann Witt, which was true. I requested that Taylor answer a few simple questions pertaining to the Witt case. Thanking him in advance for his cooperation, I signed and sealed the letter, dropped it off at the Post Office, and hoped for the best. Two weeks later, I received a five-page response from Taylor. In the first part of the letter, he wrote:

"Ms. Humphrey, I received your letter concerning the Melissa Witt case. Yes, I am aware of my name coming up in the case, even though I requested a polygraph test back during that time, it was refused by the prosecutor."

I paused, making a mental note to ask Jay C. Rider about Taylor's claim. Taylor continued,

> I think there is someone that has actually helped some coward get away with the killing of Melissa Witt and Morgan Nick. I would like very much to clear my name

and I will do anything I can to help. But first, I have a few questions for you! Have you ever heard of Detective Jay C. Rider? I would also like to know the theories and speculation of my possible involvement in these cases. Do you really want to get to the truth of all of this? Did you know that I was never questioned about the Witt murder? If you are listening to Rider, don't! Only I know the truth!

I picked up the phone and called Rider. Instead of hello, I opened the conversation with, "I received a letter from William Dillard Taylor. He asked about you and he claims he was never questioned about the Witt murder." There was an awkward pause before Rider retorted with, "Well, hello to you, too." We both laughed. Rider went on to say, "My guess is that Taylor wasn't happy that we questioned him the way we did."

"Hell, he's probably holding a grudge over being convicted for those horrible crimes he committed. There is no doubt that Taylor was questioned about the Witt murder," Rider assured me.

It's no surprise a convicted felon like Taylor would see someone like Jay C. Rider as an enemy. After all, it was Rider's full-time job to protect and serve the community by aggressively working to keep criminals like Taylor off the streets.

I continued reading Taylor's barely legible handwriting. His words laser focused on the accusations against him for child rape. Taylor was trying to convince me he was set up. "I've never hurt anyone. I'm innocent! It's all lies," he wrote.

I read through the letter once more and tossed it aside. Nothing in the letter matched up with court records. Taylor's words were nothing more than those of a vengeful convicted child rapist with a wild imagination. Over time Taylor would send a dozen more letters—each more bizarre than the first. I stopped corresponding with him in 2019 when it became clear he could not provide any useful information about Melissa's murder.

Oddly enough, William Dillard Taylor isn't the strangest character Jay C. Rider encountered while investigating the Witt case. "Believe it or not," said Rider, "we investigated a homeless man for mailing obscene sexual devices to Mary Ann Witt."

Roger Dale Wood, best known at the time for pushing a grocery cart loaded with cans and trash in downtown Fort Smith, was charged with two counts of mailing obscene packages.

Rider described the incident as "outrageous" and "the act of a sick and perverted mind." On January 18, less than a week after Melissa's body was recovered from the Ozark National Forest, a USPS employee was sorting mail when he noticed a package addressed to the Witt home. The shoebox-sized package was missing a return address. Suspicious, the employee contacted authorities, a sexual device was found inside the box.

"The package had been mailed from a drop box located at 18th and B Streets," Rider said. "Wood was attempting to frame another man for killing Melissa because he suspected the man had been stealing from him."

Rider warned Mary Ann to be on the lookout for additional packages. "And wouldn't you know it," said Rider, "on February 2, a manila envelope arrived at her home. It also contained a sexual device."

After the second package arrived, a joint investigation involving the FBI, USPS, Fort Smith and Arkansas Police led to Wood's arrest. "We had Wood under surveillance for several weeks," said Rider. "Just a sick, sick thing for him to do to anyone, especially to a grieving mother."

It turns out that Wood was no stranger to the criminal justice system. According to court records, Wood was convicted in 1985 for felony first-degree sexual abuse. He was given a five-year suspended sentence after pleading no contest. "I still find it bizarre that Wood interjected himself into the Witt case," said Rider. "But after an intense investigation, we are confident he was not responsible for Melissa's murder."

Over the span of almost three decades, Rider's tireless passion for the Witt case has brought resolution for other criminal cases. "As we looked at possible suspects for the Witt murder, we would run background investigations on them," Rider said. "That led to us discovering other offenses they committed and we would arrest them." One such arrest was of a 23-year-old Fort Smith man suspected of robbery and kidnapping. The suspect hijacked another man's car at gunpoint, robbed him, and pistol-whipped him while forcing him into the car's trunk. "Thankfully," said Rider, "we found him, arrested him, and got him off the streets."

Rider has carried Melissa's cold case with him through the years—chipping away at hundreds of leads, seeking similarities in other crime scenes, and briefing each and every new detective assigned to Melissa's case. His determined enthusiasm to catch Witt's killer is fierce. "I will not give up until this case is solved," promises Rider. I believe him. There is no doubt that Rider's analytic ability cultivated from decades of investigations of major crimes has made him a legend. It has been an absolute honor to learn from him. He has taught me everything from interpreting crime scene evidence to understanding potential motives. Most importantly, he's taught me how to withhold judgment and to approach Melissa's murder case like a chess player trying to think many moves ahead.

One afternoon, five years after our initial meeting, Rider turned the tables and began to interview me—asking why I am so passionate about Melissa's case. I launched into a complicated answer, that when I was in the fourth grade, living in southwest Oklahoma, I was in a bowling alley with my dad who played in a league, just like Melissa's mother had. While my dad bowled, a man started up a conversation with me. At some point, my dad went to the restroom and the man, who we later learned abused at least one other little girl, tried to lure my sister and me out of the bowling alley (more on that in Chapter 13).

Three years later, I moved out of that small town to Greenwood, Arkansas. During that short year in

Greenwood, I built close friendships that would last a lifetime. It turns out, many of those same friends also had a close relationship with Melissa Witt. Rider seemed to understand that my ties to Melissa are many and complex.

After I haltingly shared my reasons for my passion about Melissa Witt's case, Rider nodded, his kind eyes conveying a message of acceptance and respect.

After a few minutes, I broke the silence by tossing questions back to Rider. What was his driving force? Why was he so passionate about Melissa's case? After all, Rider was no stranger to murder. He had investigated hundreds of crimes. Why was Melissa's murder different?

"The son of a bitch that killed Melissa Witt did this in my town, on my watch as Captain of the Major Crimes Unit," Rider explained. "He needs to be brought to justice. I haven't forgotten what he did to that poor girl and I'm still coming for him."

Chapter Four
THE ALL-AMERICAN GIRL

Since 2015, I've invested a substantial amount of time seeking answers to the question "who was Melissa Ann Witt?" The news footage surrounding Melissa's murder provided few clues. Reporters consistently painted a superficial description of the "beautiful female murder victim" using words like "attractive," "talented," and "All American Girl" to depict the sum total of her life. The police reports proved to be equally incomplete. Words such as "the body," "strangulation," and "decomposition" pointed only to the tragic end of her life.

A Google search provided little more than a few Internet stories about the former cheerleader and honors student. The limited content focused primarily on how the popular teenager was loved by her entire community. Other stories mentioned Melissa's dream of becoming a dental hygienist. But I longed to know more. Who was she really? I reached out to one of Melissa's closest friends, Tara Harvel Limbird, to find out.

Tara graciously accepted my request to discuss the details of her friendship with Melissa and invited our camera crew to her office in Northwest Arkansas. Tara expressed genuine gratitude for our efforts in the decades-old murder case. During our visit, Tara shared cherished mementos, photographs, and stories about the life of her beloved friend.

"I called her Missy," Tara shared. "Missy and I met when I was five years old and she was six. I had just moved to her street and she showed up to my house one day, introduced herself, and we were, you know, best buds after that."

Tara smiled as she recalled Melissa's cheerful personality. "She always had a smile on her face," recalled Tara. "She was just a happy, good girl. She was such a joy to know."

Tara also recounted memories of riding her bicycle with Melissa throughout their neighborhood. "Missy was my outdoor friend. We loved to ride bikes. I have so many good memories of spending time with her," Tara said, sighing heavily as she fought back tears. The mood in the room shifted as we witnessed the agonizing pain Tara carried over the loss of her friend. "One of our favorite things to do was to buy candy cigarettes and ride our bikes over to Hardee's or Kentucky Fried Chicken and sit in their smoking section. We thought we were so cool while we pretended to smoke." Tara smiled softly. "But you know, we did all kinds of goofy things like that. Sometimes we would turn on a soap opera and turn the volume down really low, and we would act it out. We would come up with our own script of what was being said. It was so much fun." A single tear slid down Tara's face. The memories, while beautiful, remained a painful reminder of Melissa's tragic murder.

In the eighth grade Tara moved to Van Buren. Despite the move and change of schools, Melissa and Tara remained the best of friends. "We would spend almost every summer together at the Van Buren Pool," Tara said. "My mom would drop us off in the morning and come pick us up when the pool was closing. We had the time of our lives during the summer."

Tara was a senior in high school when Melissa enrolled at Westark Community College. After high school graduation, Tara followed in Melissa's footsteps, and she too enrolled at Westark. There, the two inseparable friends shared a biology class. "We had class every Monday, Wednesday and Friday morning together. We loved having that class together," Tara recalled.

As college students, the pair enjoyed cruising around town and giggling about their latest crush. "We were always together," she said. "And once she got her new car, the white Mitsubishi, we would cruise around everywhere together." Tara paused. "I miss her so much."

The strain of Tara's conflicting emotions as she chronicled both the joys of friendship and the pain of unthinkable loss overwhelmed her. "I remember everything about Melissa," she sobbed. "Melissa was so quirky. She was so well-liked by everyone who knew her.

Melissa didn't have any enemies. None. Everyone loved her. She had this incredible smile that lit up a room. Her eyes lit up too whenever she spoke. She was so smart and bubbly and an amazing friend. It's still so hard to believe this happened. She was such a good, good person.

"She and her mom, Mary Ann, were so close. They loved each other so much. Her mom was so protective of Melissa. Her passing was so hard on Mary Ann. Her death is so unfair. All of this is so very sad. Looking back, it's so shocking that this happened to Melissa. It's so hard to believe. I want my friend back."

My team sat in silence, giving Tara the time she needed to grieve over the soul-crushing loss of her best friend.

Then, composed and ready to resume the interview, Tara next discussed events surrounding Melissa's disappearance. "Sometime around 2:00am on Friday, December 2nd, Mary Ann called my house. I was asleep and my mom had to wake me up. She asked if I knew where Melissa was because she never came home," Tara said. "But I didn't know where she was. I mean, we were going to see each other in class on Friday morning and we had plans for Friday night, but that's all I knew. I had no idea what was going on."

The next morning, Tara was surprised to find that Melissa was not in biology class. "It was absolutely not like Missy to miss class or even stay out all night. She wasn't the type. Missy wouldn't do that to her mom. She knew her mom was protective. The situation was scary because I knew something was very wrong. Missy would not do this. Deep down I knew something incredibly bad had happened to her because this was so out of character," Tara explained.

Desperate for answers, Tara and her parents, along with dozens of volunteers, canvassed the River Valley searching for the missing teen. "We knocked on doors, we passed out posters, and we even went to see a psychic," she recalled. "When the psychic told us about a blue door with yellow writing, we searched until we found a motel in Fort Smith with blue doors and yellow letters. The psychic also told us that she was alive. That kept us going. It's what we all wanted to hear and it gave us hope. We were trying everything to get some sort of a happy ending. All we wanted to do was find Missy." But that happy ending was not to be.

Tara looked away from the camera as she shared how she learned about the gruesome discovery in Franklin County. "I remember the day I got the call that a body had been found in the Ozark National Forest. Authorities thought it could be Missy and they were going to check dental records to see if it was her. That day started off so beautifully and then the temperature suddenly dropped and it began to rain—it just wouldn't stop raining that day. Looking back, I guess we all knew that the body was Missy. It was just so hard to accept." Her memories, raw and painful, echoed my own recollection of that day.

My thoughts drifted to January 13, 1995 and the sound of the evening news anchor anxiously announcing, "A body has been found in Franklin County and the question is, is the body that of Melissa Witt?" I stood motionless in the doorway of my small one-bedroom apartment trying to make sense of the situation. Why would her body be in the Ozark National Forest? Wasn't she abducted from Fort Smith? I grabbed a map of Arkansas to gauge the distance between the two locations. 60 miles. Perplexed, I sank into my blue leather couch and grabbed the remote. As I scanned television channels, finding coverage of the O.J. Simpson trial, my thoughts lingered on Melissa Witt.

As that memory replayed in my mind, Tara and I locked eyes. She cautiously shared her feelings. "It just didn't feel real. I mean, it didn't seem possible it could be her. I remember when my mom sat me down and told me that it *was* Missy's body—that dental records had confirmed it was her—I just felt numb. I remember going to the funeral at Grand Avenue Baptist Church, which was right down the street from where we had played our entire life. I remember sitting there and it still didn't feel real until the pastor said, 'Melissa Ann Witt was born on April 20th, 1975.' At that moment, hearing him say her full name and her date of birth, it all hit me. It was real. This really happened."

A few weeks after my interview with Tara Limbird, I sat in the conference room of the Fort Smith Police Department reading through Melissa's case files. A report from the Arkansas State Crime Laboratory caught my eye. I stared at the cold words on the title page: Medical Examiner Division. Case No: ME-42-95. Name: Witt, Melissa. Manner of Death: Homicide. The ten-page detailed report was divided into sections that documented everything from Melissa's blood type and the weight and appearance of her internal organs to a postmortem toxicology summary that indicated no drugs were detected in her body tissues. Page ten, entitled "Opinion," summarized the medical examiner's findings. "It is our opinion that Melissa Witt, a 19-year-old white female, died from asphyxia due to strangulation. She was found approximately 20 miles north of Ozark off Highway 23 in the Ozark National Forest at approximately 10:00am on 1-13-95. She was pronounced dead at 1:00pm on the same date. The victim was found in a wooded area by a trapper who checks the property every day. It appears that the victim had been placed behind a large rock and covered with pine needles and leaves at one time."

As I closed the report, one of Tara Limbird's last comments from our interview came to mind. "You know, sometimes I log on to Facebook and I come across people who I went to elementary school or junior high with. I see pictures of their family and their life and I see that they are doing well. I always think to myself, you know, I wonder who Missy would have married. Where would she have worked? Would she be at a dental office? Would she still be in Fort Smith? Would she have kids? Sometimes it makes me feel guilty. I mean, I have a nice life, a nice husband, a wonderful daughter..." Tara trailed off, thinking of the possibilities Then she continued, "And well, that opportunity was stolen from Missy. It's just not right." The magnitude of Tara's statement clawed at my heart. Tara was right. Melissa's killer stole so much from so many people.

As I sorted through dozens of file folders, I noticed one marked "Mary Ann Witt." Inside, I discovered a beautiful letter she had written about her daughter.

> Melissa was a good girl. She was so loving and so kind. She was truly a good soul. I never had serious trouble with Melissa. We were mother and daughter, best of friends, and a source of love and comfort for one another. I was almost 40 years old when [I had] Melissa Ann. I had waited my entire life to have that sweet angel. And now she has been taken from me. Captain Rider, please help me find who murdered my sweet, sweet girl.

The emotion behind her words broke my heart, but their power also fueled my unrelenting passion to uncover the identity of the evil monster that destroyed so many lives on that December 1, 1994.

Determined, I kept digging through the case files until I came across a bulky manila envelope. I asked Detective Williams, the lead on Melissa's murder case at the time, if I could open it. He consented. The contents of that envelope changed my life in ways that are difficult to articulate. Inside, I found crime scene photos from the Ozark National Forest. To honor Melissa's memory, I will not describe the graphic images that I saw that afternoon. What I will share is this: Those photographs displayed one of the most terrible acts of human cruelty I have ever witnessed.

Shaken, I took a break from the case files and drove to the dental office of Dr. Terry Jennings where Melissa had been employed. At the clinic, I was greeted by the Office Manager, Anita Dodson. "I've been with the dental clinic since 1992," she grinned. Anita graciously agreed to talk to me about her relationship with Melissa. "She was such a good girl and a hard worker. She got along with co-workers and patients—really with everyone she met."

Anita offered me bottled water as she shared her experience of working with Melissa. "I've worked at this clinic for a long time. I started off as a receptionist and worked my way up to the position I have now as the Office Manager. So, as you can imagine, I knew Melissa very well," she said. "In fact, I called her Missy instead of Melissa. She was a dental assistant for us and she was good at her job. She wanted to go to dental hygiene school. Melissa had all kinds of plans for her life. She was such an amazing person. Everyone loved her."

Anita laughed as she recalled fond memories of her time working with the young college student. "Melissa loved to joke around and we loved to joke around with her. Several times when it was payday, I would pretend we didn't have a paycheck for her. Missy's reaction was always so cute and funny. I really do miss her."

According to Anita, the dynamics in the dental clinic changed after Melissa's disappearance. "The staff here are close, like family, and we did all we could to support each other when Missy was missing. We were all just so hopeful that she would be found and come back to us. Once we knew, you know, that her body was found, well, it was a very hard time," Anita shared. "Everyone was upset for such a long time. I just can't understand anyone wanting to hurt Missy. She was so sweet and so nice."

While Anita and I sat in her office discussing the tragic loss of a life gone too soon, Dr. Jennings asked if he could meet with me before his next patient arrived. He shook my hand and thanked me for taking the time to visit his office. Then he offered up his thoughts on Melissa's murder. "The case is baffling and heartbreaking. Missy was a great employee and a great person. I just can't imagine who would do something like this to that sweet girl. But I hope your efforts will bring closure. We all want to know who did this to her. She deserves justice."

Before I left, Anita shared photos of Melissa taken during her time at the dental office. The happy, smiling photos were a vast contrast to the horrific crime scene images I had seen earlier in the day. Why would someone brutally murder such a kind, generous, and loving young woman? I could feel the lump in my throat promising to betray my calm and collected professional appearance. My internal struggle came to a screeching halt as Anita leaned toward me and whispered the words, "Please find the monster that did this." With calm confidence, I looked Anita in the eye and I squeezed her hand. "Law enforcement will find him. They're going to get him. I promise. And I will not stop until that happens." We said our goodbyes, and Anita hugged me as I walked out the door.

I could hear birds singing in the distance as I stepped outside the dental office into the sunshine. My steps were heavy, my every thought was on Melissa. I walked slowly to my car. It was hard to comprehend that this parking lot was one of the last places Melissa had been seen alive. Images of the gruesome crime scene photos continued to haunt me. Overcome with emotion, I hurried to unlock my car. As I shakily put my keys in the ignition, a red cardinal circled overhead and landed on my left side view mirror. Hot tears slid down my face as I watched the beautiful bird. I was reminded of the many hours I spent as a young girl, birdwatching with my grandfather. I could vividly recall him teaching me that a cardinal symbolizes beauty in the midst of darkness and hope in the midst of sorrow. He also once told me that when a cardinal lands nearby, it represents the presence of someone who has departed this world. I started the car, and as the engine quietly hummed, I watched the bird gracefully flap its wings and fly off before landing on the roof of the dental office. Instead of driving away, I sat in the parking lot and wept.

Chapter Five
SMALL TOWN SECRETS

Nestled in the Ozark Mountains, Fort Smith is the second largest city in Arkansas after Little Rock. In 1994, the population barely exceeded 73,000 compared to Little Rock's 176,000. The picturesque small-town, surrounded by mountains, river valleys, forests, lakes, and bayous, beckoned those longing for a simpler life.

Established in 1817 as a western frontier military post, Fort Smith lies on the Arkansas-Oklahoma border at the Belle Point juncture of the Arkansas and Poteau rivers. The town was named after General Thomas Adams Smith, commander of the United States Army Rifle Regiment. As Fort Smith grew, so did its reputation as a community overrun with brothels, saloons, outlaws, and crime. In its early years, the city was out of control and the United States Attorney for the Western District of Arkansas, William Henry Harrison Clayton, recognized the need for a strong judge to bring law and order to the citizens of Fort Smith. To do that, Clayton enlisted the help of his brother and the former governor of Arkansas, U.S. Senator Powell Clayton. Together, the two organized the appointment of U.S. District Judge Isaac Parker.

Judge Parker served in that position from 1875 to 1896. During his first term in office, Parker was nicknamed the "Hanging Judge," after sentencing 8 murderers to death. Over the span of his career in Fort Smith, Judge Parker sentenced 160 people to death and executed 79 of those on the gallows. His courthouse is forever marked as a National Historic Site where "more men were put to death by the U.S. Government than in any other place in American history."

The City of Fort Smith continued to grow steadily until the onset of the Great Depression. Interestingly, between 1907 and 1924, Fort Smith gained notoriety as one of the few cities in U.S. history to legalize and regulate prostitution, albeit limited to a restricted area of Fort Smith known as "The Row." The decision to legalize prostitution resulted in more than the community bargained for when the crime rates for drugs, domestic violence, and homicide drastically increased. Later, the rough and tough city of Fort Smith would even entice the infamous criminal duo Bonnie Parker and Clyde Barrow to use it as a hideout to evade capture from law enforcement.

Despite the rise of crime, Fort Smith continued to grow, and so did its diverse population. Beginning in 1975, Fort Chaffee, originally built to serve as both a training camp and a Prisoner-of-War camp, became the federal resettlement location of Vietnamese refugees who fled their country after the fall of Saigon. Eventually, many of those refugees chose to settle in Fort Smith permanently. Later, Hispanic immigrants, along with hundreds of Laotian men, women, and children, followed suit and made their home in Fort Smith. At the same time, companies such as the Whirlpool Corporation moved in and stimulated the economic growth of the city. The opening of both the St. Edward Mercy Medical Center (renamed Mercy Fort Smith in 2012) and the Central Mall, at the time one of the largest indoor shopping malls in Arkansas, also contributed to the tremendous growth Fort Smith eventually experienced. In spite of the rapidly growing cultural and economic landscape, one thing remained the same: Fort Smith had developed a strong reputation for criminal activity and, as a result, some very unsavory characters made the city their home.

Among those unsavory characters was a man named George Kent Wallace who moved to Fort Smith in 1986. Four years later, in December, 1990, Wallace was arrested and charged with kidnapping and the attempted murder of Ross Allen Ferguson. According to police reports, Ferguson was picked up in a grocery store parking lot in Van Buren, Arkansas by a man posing as law enforcement. After he was stabbed six times, Ferguson pretended to be dead in order to escape his captor. Wallace was arrested later that evening in the same area where the abduction had occurred. Hours later, shaken but determined, Ferguson identified George Kent Wallace in a lineup.

After his arrest, another victim, James Branson, came forward and told authorities that Wallace, posing as law enforcement, had kidnapped him and taken him to a pond in Le Flore County, Oklahoma. Wallace shackled and handcuffed Branson but eventually set him free because of Branson's constant kicking and screaming. Another young man, Isidro Hernandez also came forward. He reported a similar story of a man posing as a law enforcement officer who tried to pick him up. According to Hernandez, he was able to talk his way out of going anywhere with Wallace.

Ten days later, the body of twelve-year-old Alonzo Don Cade was found in a pit near Fort Chaffee. Cade had last been seen at a Westark Community College basketball game on November 24, 1990. After the discovery, Wallace was questioned about Cade, and about two other bodies found in a Le Flore County pond. Marky Anthony McLaughlin, 14, and William Eric Domer, 15, had both been shot in the back of the head with a small-caliber weapon. Wallace confessed and was eventually convicted and sentenced to three life-in-prison terms, plus sixty years for the murders of McLaughlin and Domer, and for the abduction and attempted murder of Ferguson. Wallace remains the prime suspect in Alonzo Don Cade's unsolved murder.

Before moving to Fort Smith, Wallace lived in North Carolina, where his criminal record dated back to 1966. Wallace was nicknamed locally as the "Mad Paddler" because he allegedly impersonated law enforcement officers in order to lure teenagers into his car, then, once inside, Wallace would handcuff and paddle the teens. In prison, Wallace confessed to the murders of Jeffrey Lee Foster and Thomas Steward Reed, both from North Carolina. While he was never prosecuted for those deaths, he remains the main suspect in their murders.

On Thursday, August 10, 2000, George Kent Wallace was executed by lethal injection by the state of Oklahoma. We may never know how many additional unconfessed crimes Wallace carried to the grave.

Wallace, however, wasn't the only man in Fort Smith impersonating law enforcement. According to news reports, Connie Bowen told police that Douglas Lawrence Logan threatened to arrest her unless he was allowed to drive her home from Club Fouquets in Fort Smith. Police said Logan claimed Bowen had been drinking and he was only offering her a ride home.

Logan had allegedly been following Bowen at the bar and offered to take her and a friend out for a cup of coffee, then drive them home. Outside the bar they argued and Logan tried to convince Bowen he was a police officer. Bowen said Logan ordered her to get into her car. She complied, fearing she would go to jail if she didn't agree. For that crime, Logan was arrested near the parking lot from where Melissa Witt had disappeared. As part of the Melissa Witt murder investigation, law enforcement searched Logan's car and brought him in for questioning on three separate occasions. To date, investigators have been unsuccessful in their attempts to find a connection between Logan and Melissa's murder.

Curious about Logan, I tracked him down in South Dakota to ask him a few questions. We spoke on the phone briefly and he told me that he remembers being questioned in the Witt case, but denied having any involvement in her disappearance or murder. I asked Logan to elaborate on some information that I had uncovered about him. I asked if he was willing to discuss his July 30, 1985 conviction for felony sexual contact with a minor under age 16. Logan replied, "So what if I did that? What's there to say?" Shocked at Logan's defiant response, I asked him to explain why, along with his criminal charges, his public online sex offender registration included the screen names "Samurai" and "Midnight Vampire." Logan's response was shocking. He cursed at me and screamed, "Who the fuck cares what screen names I use to talk to young girls online?! Their parents should watch them better if they don't want them talking to me!" Then he hung up.

One afternoon, as I was talking to Jay C. Rider, I told him about my conversation with Douglas Logan. "I'm not surprised," said Rider. "Guys like Logan make a career out of preying on women and children. It's disgusting. I've seen much worse though. Have I ever told you about Charles Ray Vines?"

Charles Ray Vines, now deceased, served life without parole in the Arkansas Department of Correction for two murders: Juanita Wofford of Fort Smith in 1993 and Ruth Henderson of Crawford County in 1995. Law enforcement linked Vines to the murders after he was caught raping a 16-year-old Crawford County girl in 2000. According to

Rider, Vines also admitted to raping an elderly Fort Smith woman in 1993, just months before he raped and killed Juanita Wofford. As part of his confession, Vines admitted to having sex with his victims once they were dead. It was reported he told one officer, "That's my favorite kind of sex… the kind with dead women. It's what I fantasize about."

According to Jay C. Rider, most people in the community respected Vines and thought he was a good person. "The crazy thing about all of this," said Rider, "is that Vines seemed 'normal.' People described him as being the best neighbor and an all-around great guy. Most everyone he knew had great things to say about him. They had no idea he was a monster." When Vines was arrested for the attempted rape of the young teenager, DNA evidence from that crime scene was a perfect match for DNA in both murder cases. "It was a relief we caught the guy," said Rider. "There is just no telling who else he might have hurt or killed."

Shortly after his arrest, Vines was questioned about his involvement in other crimes, including the murder of Melissa Witt. "I spent five days, eight hours at a time, with Vines," Rider said. "He talked about some horrible things he had done. But he was adamant that he didn't kill Melissa."

After my conversation with Rider, I wrote to Charles Ray Vines in prison. In my letter, I introduced myself and explained my passion for the Witt case. Surprisingly, Vines wrote back almost immediately. Before his death in

2019, Vines and I exchanged dozens of letters. He talked about finding Jesus Christ while in prison, and he often expressed remorse for the crimes he had committed. He wrote:

> Ms. Humphrey, I am a changed man. Jesus has forgiven me. I did some terrible, terrible things. But that's behind me now. I am in prison paying the price for the choices I made. I can live with that. As far as the Witt girl, I had nothing to do with that. If I was involved, I would admit it. There is no use keeping that kind of thing a secret. I did not kill her. You are persistent so keep pushing to find her killer. I think you will do it.
>
> Sincerely, Charlie.

I shared the letter from Vines with Jay C. Rider. "He's told you the truth. Vines did do some terrible things. In fact, his crimes involved some of the worst violence I have ever seen," said Rider. "I spent over 40 hours extensively interviewing Vines. We talked about his crimes and we talked about many unsolved cases but, after interviewing Vines, I do not believe he killed Melissa Witt. I just don't believe he's our guy."

It's frightening to think that Vines lived and worked in Fort Smith for years before his crimes caught up with him. But Vines wasn't the only predator living in Fort Smith and leading a secret life. In 1995, Nathaniel Bar-Jonah, born David Paul Brown, was a convicted felon and alleged cannibal who came to Arkansas to live with a single woman and her young children that he met through a classified ad. The unsuspecting single mother had no idea that Bar-Jonah was a card-carrying member of the National Man/Boy Love Association, also known as NAMBLA. The vast majority of NAMBLA members are men that have a sexual preference for young boys. However, many of their members are pedophiles that will molest and rape any child, regardless of their gender.

Six years after leaving Arkansas, Nathaniel Bar-Jonah was arrested for the 1996 murder of Zachary Ramsey. Authorities believe that Bar-Jonah raped the young boy, murdered him, and then ate his remains. While searching Bar-Jonah's home, law enforcement discovered human remains in his garage of a young boy between the ages of 9-14. Authorities also discovered thousands of pictures of young boys along with encrypted writings. Once decoded by the FBI, it was found that those writings included recipes entitled "Little Boy Pot Pie" and "Little Boy Stew."

Authorities next investigated Bar-Jonah's movements across the United States and found evidence that he had traveled to Arkansas, Colorado, Florida, Massachusetts, Michigan, and Washington. A full-scale effort to review missing children reports in those states was launched. To date, I can find no evidence that findings from that investigation have been made available to the public.

In researching Nathaniel Bar-Jonah, I discovered that he was released from custody in July of 1991 after a Suffolk Superior Court judge in Massachusetts took the word of two psychologists who said he was no longer a threat to society. At that time, a loophole existed in the state sentencing laws. Inmates with good behavior were granted 12.5 days off their sentence for every month served. Because Bar-Jonah was a model inmate, he walked out of prison five years early. Less than a month later, he assaulted a boy in Oxford, Massachusetts. He was given only a two-year *suspended* sentence for that crime.

It is believed that Bar-Jonah could be responsible for dozens of additional crimes across the United States. I've always wondered if he had any involvement in the abduction of six-year-old Morgan Nick from Alma, Arkansas. Morgan was abducted from a Little League game on June 9, 1995, six months after Melissa disappeared. The distance between Alma and Fort Smith is only eighteen miles, which makes it a plausible theory (at least in my mind) that the child predator, and NAMBLA member, could have been involved with Morgan's abduction. Bar-Jonah, an opportunist, preyed on both male and female children.

Unfortunately, Nathaniel Bar-Jonah refused to talk about any of the crimes he committed.

On April 13, 2008, Bar-Jonah was found unresponsive in his prison cell. A myocardial infarction was determined to be the cause of death. Like George Kent Wallace, Bar-Jonah carried his secrets to the grave.

In 1995, nine months after Melissa Witt was abducted and murdered, a woman named Lori Murchison went missing. Murchison had been jailed along with her boyfriend on a public intoxication charge. She was released on September 2. Murchison told jail officials she planned to pick up her paycheck at the Oaks Lodge Nursing Home and come back to bail out her boyfriend. Murchison never returned. In fact, she never picked up her paycheck. She was last seen alive at the office of the Continental Motel where she had stopped to retrieve the key to her room.

According to the Fort Smith Police Department, Murchison, who is presumed dead, is still listed as a missing person. To complicate matters, the Sebastian County prosecuting attorney at the time, Ron Fields, became a suspect in her murder. Rumors spread like wildfire that Ron Fields had Murchison killed after she allegedly made statements that linked him to drug trafficking. The FBI was called in to investigate and eventually a grand jury was convened. As you might imagine, the unfounded allegations deeply impacted Fields' career. In May 2005, officials at the Department of Homeland Security notified Fields that his security clearance had been revoked and he was suspended from his job. Fields appealed the suspension and lost.

The former Marine and Vietnam Veteran didn't allow the scandal to keep him down for long. Fields took his experience as the former Deputy Prosecuting Attorney for Sebastian County from 1972 to 1975, and his nine terms as Prosecuting Attorney for Sebastian County, and went into private practice. There, Fields has proven to be incredibly savvy at handling legal matters involving everything from illegal drugs, possession, and assault to capital offenses. His unparalleled legal skills have garnered

Fields the distinction of being one of the top criminal defense lawyers in the state of Arkansas.

According to statements made on record by Ron Lockhart, a former Fort Smith police detective and the man who led the investigation into Murchison's disappearance, the allegations against Fields are false. Lockhart is on record as stating that he believes Murchison died of an accidental drug overdose and that her body was disposed of by someone who was with her when she died. Whether that theory is true or not, Lori Murchison's case, like Melissa Witt's, remains unsolved.

The horrific crimes happening in Fort Smith in the 1990s don't stop there. A 21-year-old man named Jonathan Keith Cole was convicted in September 2000 for the 1996 murder of Summer Wilkinson of Fort Smith. Wilkinson's remains were later discovered in Oklahoma near a racetrack.

Cole was convicted of Wilkinson's death while already serving a 70-year sentence in Arkansas for his conviction in the 1997 murder of 13-year-old Lisa Teague. She was also from Fort Smith. The remains of the young teenager were discovered in a vacant lot. Cole and three other men allegedly picked Wilkinson up from her home and then raped and beat her to death before stabbing her multiple times. Her body was then dumped near the Tri-State Speedway in Pocola, Oklahoma.

Investigators aggressively questioned Cole in the Witt murder, but there was no evidence of his involvement in the crime.

I kept asking myself the same question as I researched the history of Fort Smith: What is it about this place and horrific crime? I am still not sure I have the answer. What I do know is that a foreboding darkness inhabited that small town. Like a twilight shadow, evil crept across the city, silently watching and waiting for its next victim.

When that sinister force snatched Melissa Witt on December 1, 1994, it shook the town to its core. Her murder shattered the illusion that Fort Smith was a safe, peaceful, white-picket-fence community. The sleepy little town was now wide awake, and it would never be the same.

Chapter Six
CONSPIRACY THEORIES

I discovered early on in the Melissa Witt investigation that her cold case, like so many others, is rife with rumors and conflict. For years now, an army of conspiracy theorists have regularly filled my inbox with conflicting theories, stories, and false leads about Melissa's abduction and murder. One conspiracy theorist, however, stands out among all the rest—a woman I will refer to as "Sandy Jones."

Sandy first contacted me in early 2016 via email. The subject line of her message, "I was a close friend of Melissa Witt," caught my attention so I immediately responded. However, it didn't take long after speaking with Sandy on the phone to realize that this woman had never been close friends with Melissa. Instead, Sandy was a patient at the dental clinic where Melissa had worked and the two women were, at best, no more than casual acquaintances.

Despite the initial red flag from Sandy's exaggerated story about the nature of her relationship with Melissa,

I continued to correspond with her. My conversations with Sandy were interesting. Like me, she had a deep passion for true crime. As a lifetime resident of the River Valley, Sandy had amassed a wealth of information about dozens of unsolved crimes in the area, and this made our conversations incredibly intriguing.

After a few months of these back-and-forth discussions regarding unsolved crimes in Fort Smith, Sandy suddenly dropped a bomb one afternoon when she blurted out, "Look, I have information about the man who murdered Melissa. I know who did it."

"Wh… what?" I stammered. "Where did you get this information?" I asked.

"I will tell you," she said, "in due time. But I can't yet. It isn't safe."

Over the next several weeks, Sandy continued to drop hints about the "important information" she had discovered about Melissa's murder. Frustrated, overwhelmed, and unwilling to participate in her game of cat and mouse, I pressed Sandy hard for answers. Reluctantly, she finally shared her outrageous story with me. According to Sandy, a strange cast of characters were involved in a conspiracy to cover up the teenager's brutal death.

"You're telling me," I said slowly, "that Melissa's murder involves high stakes gambling, a prominent local businessman, corrupt public officials, and a missing child from Alma, Arkansas?"

"Yes, that's exactly what I am telling you," Sandy replied. "It's true. I even have a recording to prove it."

I let out a long sigh. Even though I had serious doubts about the reliability of her story, I encouraged her to contact law enforcement. "All right then, Sandy. You need to reach out to law enforcement to share this information and to let them hear the recording. I can help you set up an appointment with the lead on Melissa's case. His name is Detective Williams."

Sandy's quick retort surprised me. "You don't want to hear the recording?" she sneered.

"Yes, of course I do, but only after you have taken it to Detective Williams. Let's see what he has to say first," I replied.

A week later my phone rang. "LaDonna, it's Detective Williams. Do you have a few minutes to talk?" he asked.

"Of course. How can I help you?"

"Well," he paused and then asked, "how well do you know Sandy Jones?"

"Not well at all," I said. "We recently started talking in connection with the Melissa Witt case. But I've never even met her in person."

Detective Williams chuckled. "She's definitely got quite a story to tell, doesn't she? And she's under the impression that the two of you are the best of friends."

"Best of friends?" I repeated.

"The BEST of friends," he assured me.

The phone was silent for a few moments before we both erupted in laughter. "Oh boy," I finally replied. "What have I stepped into?"

The Detective went on to describe that during his meeting with Sandy, she provided a myriad of details about the man she insists killed Melissa. In fact, she went as far as to implicate this man in a series of other crimes, including child abduction, drug trafficking, and extortion. Sandy's accusations, like her imagination, were limitless.

༄

It didn't take long before a very irritated Sandy also called.

"Hello?" I answered cautiously.

"That Detective Williams," she immediately complained, "he made me wait on him forever and then he didn't take anything I said seriously! Can you believe that?"

"Hi, Sandy," I replied. "I am sorry you feel that way. I know he takes every potential lead in Melissa's case very seriously. Give him a chance to work through the information you gave him. He wants to solve Melissa's case. Just give it some time," I said.

Sandy scoffed loudly at my comment. "What is this?" she angrily demanded. "So now you're part of the cover up?" The phone disconnected.

Stunned by her cold remarks, I sat in silence. "What just happened?" I thought. The answer came sooner than I expected. Within minutes, my cell phone buzzed, and with it a long diatribe text from Sandy. Her conspiracy theory had expanded and included a new player: me.

Unfortunately, Sandy's hateful and accusatory message was not the last of our contact. She could not, it turns out, move past her insatiable desire to viciously interject herself into Melissa's case. Her venom trickled in ever so slowly through the creation of dozens of anonymous emails and messages sent through fake social media accounts. The overall message was always the same: There was a large conspiracy to cover-up the "truth" behind the murder of Melissa Witt.

After several months of her harassment, Sandy's efforts drastically escalated. One afternoon as I sat in an important meeting, I received an urgent text from Jay C. Rider. "LaDonna, could you give me a call? We need to talk about something important," he wrote. "I've been receiving some strange text messages," he continued.

Concerned, I stepped outside to call Rider. "What's going on?" I asked.

"Well," he laughed nervously, "I've received some strange and salacious text messages that you should know about. The messages are about you."

"About me?" I questioned.

"Yes. These texts are both crude and ridiculous," he said. His voice hinted at both embarrassment and disappointment.

"Sure, okay," I replied. "I'd like to know what is going on."

Over the next fifteen minutes Rider described the graphic nature of the text messages. I was shocked, embarrassed, and angry. "This is going to sound random, but I'm curious…. Do you happen to know a woman named Sandy Jones?" I asked.

Rider paused. "Sandy Jones? Yes, actually, I do," he said. "She recently contacted me about a cold case in Fort Smith. Do you know her?"

"Do I know her?" I laughed. "She's the one behind that crazy conspiracy theory in the Witt case. These text messages have to be from her," I reasoned. "I would bet money on it."

We finished our phone call and agreed not to give Sandy the attention she so desperately craved. "Time is a precious and a limited commodity," Rider said, "and if we want to find the identity of Melissa Witt's killer, we can't afford to get sidetracked by Sandy Jones."

Ignoring Sandy's psychotic behavior, however, proved to be a difficult task. She went out of her way to contact law enforcement, respected journalists, retired professionals, and the general public with her grandiose stories of corruption. Chasing down the false leads and information Sandy generates has proven to be a tremendous and exhausting waste of time and energy.

In some cases, the actions of zealous true crime enthusiasts like Sandy can have devastating consequences not only for a cold case but for the personal lives of the people associated with it. Every second spent sifting through the abyss of make-believe information that people like Sandy dole out under fake identities takes precious time away from investigating real leads in Melissa's case. Sandy's verbal assaults and insults directed at my documentary team, law enforcement, and me personally has taken its toll. And while our dedication to solving Melissa's murder keeps my team focused and determined, there are definitely days we question our ability to continue to cope with the dark side of human nature that people like Sandy Jones represent.

Fortunately, Jay C. Rider has used this experience as an opportunity to teach my team some valuable lessons. "It's always important, especially in a cold case," Rider said, "to ask yourself these questions when tips come in: Where did the tip come from? Can it be believed? What important resources and man hours are required to follow up on this information? And finally, what information do we already have on file that can be cross-matched with the new tip?"

Rider's wisdom has proven to be invaluable in assisting us in recognizing a real tip vs. Sandy's latest effort to derail the important work we are trying to accomplish. For example, when a local news editor contacted me to discuss a series of Facebook messages he received from "a local homeless woman named Annie claiming to have valuable information in the Witt investigation," I immediately suspected that Sandy Jones had struck once again!

According to the editor, the tipster claimed to be a disabled woman named Annie, who lived in a van near the Fort Smith Riverfront trail. "In my entire career," the editor said, "I've never heard this kind of a story. It's unbelievably jaw-dropping."

As he relayed the information, I was aghast. Despite changes in minor details, the crux of the story remained: conspiracy, corruption, and cover-up. Sandy's frightening fixation on creating a narrative centered on an imaginary conspiracy had crossed the line from obsessive to exploitative, and was completely distasteful.

After the "Annie" incident, Sandy suddenly went radio silent. I suspect the involvement of law enforcement,

IT professionals, and our legal team helped aid in her decision to quietly disappear. But the damage was done. Sandy's actions left an indelible mark on each of us, giving us a new definition of what a monster can be: a vindictive, internet-troll-mastermind set on destruction.

The majority of true crime consumers that read the books, listen to the podcasts, and watch the documentaries are women. A rare few, like Sandy, however, become more than just passive observers. They take their obsessions a step further to interject themselves into the story. These types of people are driven, almost instinctively, to replicate a version of the chaos they have greedily devoured as part of their true crime fascination.

I suspect if we could see inside Sandy's mind, we might discover an incredibly complex and romanticized view of murder and mayhem. Maybe we would also discover that Sandy, and others like her, thrive on these narratives as a way to cope with the parts of themselves that society won't accept—those parts that receive great pleasure from the pain and torment of other human beings.

The truth is that no one may ever fully understand what fueled Sandy Jones' obsession to interject herself into the Melissa Witt case. The experience will forever leave me questioning every tip we receive: "Is this real? Could this be Sandy?"

Chapter Seven
DIARY CONFESSIONS

I bounced my leg nervously as I sat in the quiet, cramped cubicle inside the Fort Smith Police Department. Detective Williams broke the silence by offering me a cup of coffee. I smiled, nodded, and thanked him for the kind gesture. Minutes later, he placed a warm Styrofoam cup in my hand. The aroma emanating from the cup was strong and sour. I cautiously sipped the dark, muddy substance and immediately regretted my decision as the thick liquid hit my stomach with a thud. I winced and stared into the cup. "It's heavy and bitter, but it will definitely wake you up," Detective Williams promised. Instead of being polite and drinking the rest of the coffee, I ceremoniously placed the cup on the table and pushed it out of reach.

Indifferent about my refusal to drink the bitter brew, Detective Williams laughed and leaned across his desk to retrieve a small spiralbound notebook from the top drawer. "Well, we might as well let you get started," he said. My stomach churned nervously as he placed the 5 x 8 Stuart Hall notebook on the table directly in front of me. I held my breath and ran my fingers across the blue and pink cover. This wasn't just any notebook. It was a diary. And it had belonged to Melissa Ann Witt.

As I stared at the notebook, I longed to read the stories Melissa had penned of the collected memories that made up her life. But I couldn't bring myself to open it. As I grappled with my emotions, I thought about my own diary. In it, I kept detailed notes on everything from my first crush to my painful and volatile relationship with my estranged mother. The diary, a sacred possession, is hidden away in my closet. It's meant for my eyes only. I can only assume that Melissa felt the same way. Conflicted, I sat in silence. How could I trespass into Melissa's private thoughts?

"It was hard at first," Detective Williams offered, sensing my struggle. "It is difficult to read someone's private thoughts and feelings without their permission. But you will learn a lot by reading that diary. I did" he promised. "Melissa was a good kid. Very innocent. Very sweet." He reached across the table, picked up the diary, and randomly chose a passage to read aloud: "I have tonsillitis, but I am taking medication for it. Anyway, momma got me a new car stereo. Aunt Helen gave me fifty dollars. Daddy gave me twenty dollars and I got some cards." Detective Williams paused and handed me the open diary. The entry was dated April 21,1994, one day after Melissa's 19th birthday. I began reading where

Detective Williams left off: "It is now 2:15 a.m. and I have to go to school and work today. I just cannot go to sleep. I'm not sure if it's the medication I'm taking or what, but I hope I'm ok tomorrow. Gotta go! Melissa." I quickly shut the diary and closed my eyes. The mystery and intrigue of reading Melissa's personal history was compelling and I knew Detective Williams was right. I would learn so much about Melissa by reading her diary. Casting my uncertainty aside, I took a deep breath, opened my eyes, and dived in.

Over the next hour, I became engrossed in the personal thoughts, feelings, and everyday experiences of Melissa Ann Witt. I laughed aloud at her silly stories and my heart sank over her disappointments. I felt a deeper connection to Melissa that afternoon. Flipping through the pages of her diary felt like visiting an old friend—it was both magical and heartbreaking. As I neared the end of the journal, I felt a deep ache in my chest. It was hard to accept that such a beautiful life had been cut so short.

After reading the last page, I gently closed the book, stood up, and thanked Detective Williams for his time. "Can I come back in a few weeks to go through the files and read the diary again?" I asked. Detective Williams nodded his head in agreement. I started down the hallway but didn't get very far before I turned back and asked, "Do you think her killer's name is in that diary?" Detective Williams' facial expression turned serious as he thought about my question. "I think there is a great probability the name of her killer is in that diary," he said. "I really do think that diary is important. I'm glad you read it," he added. I smiled, shook his hand again, and walked out the door. As I drove back to Northwest Arkansas, my thoughts remained on Melissa, her diary, and the person who had murdered her.

Once at home, I hastily fumbled with a stepladder to reach a box that was hidden away on the top shelf in my closet. Inside, I found my own diary. The glossy white book, decorated with a small purple butterfly, contained a decade and a half of both cherished and painful memories. As I quickly thumbed through the pages, one particular entry took me by surprise. On Friday, January 20th, 1995, I wrote, "Absolutely hate the new class schedule. My hope is that I can get it changed next week. Everything else seems to be going smoothly. It's sad but I think everyone is focused on the news from Fort Smith. Last week, Melissa Witt's body was discovered in the Ozark National Forest. Such a sad, sad ending. I wonder what happened. She was so young. I can't believe she was murdered!" I was stunned. I had no recollection of writing this entry two decades earlier.

Two weeks after reading her diary for the first time, I returned to the Fort Smith Police Department with my documentary crew. As the team prepared to sort through Melissa's case files, I sat across the room at an empty table. I placed my diary next to Melissa's. I was curious if any of our journal entries were written during the same time frame. To my amazement, in what turned out to be the last week of Melissa Witt's life, we each wrote the following five diary entries on the exact same days, a time when we were both in school, but me as a 21-year-old newlywed, and her as a still carefree and fresh-faced teenager.

November 13th, 1994

Melissa: Last night, we went to Fayetteville. We had a pretty good time. We spent time with friends and we played football with them. After football, we watched TV. We had fun! At least I did.

LaDonna: We moved into our new apartment in Springdale. It's so tiny! How will we ever fit a Christmas tree into this space? I am so ready to go Christmas tree shopping and buy ornaments for our very own tree!

November 20th, 1994

Melissa: I had the best time this weekend. Actually, it's a long story but we did watch Aspen Extreme.

LaDonna: We bought a REAL Christmas tree. It's huge and it takes up most of the living room in the apartment. Pine needles are everywhere! We love the tree but we are definitely going to invest in a fake tree for next year. This has been a total pain.

November 22, 1994

Melissa: Today was an OK day. I went to school and work and that was about it. Got to go, Melissa.

LaDonna: Homework is overwhelming. I won't be writing much thanks to my Greek Lit. class!

November 27, 1994

Melissa: Today wasn't such a good day for me. I woke up this morning sick as a dog and I threw up and then I had fever and aching and chills all day. I don't know how I got this, but I hope it doesn't last too long.

LaDonna: I have zero time to keep a diary anymore. School, work and being a newlywed is time consuming!

November 28, 1994

Melissa: My kitty died tonight. I am so sad. He's been sick for a very long time. Tonight, he crawled into his litter box and just laid down. A couple of hours later, mama moved him under his blanket. I cried a little bit, but at least I know he's in kitty heaven.

LaDonna: It's time to start Christmas shopping! I can't wait. I love this time of the year! Is it silly to dream of a White Christmas? I hope we are able to make the Silver Dollar City trip with our church. I hear the Christmas lights are beautiful this time of year.

The painful task of reading the contrasting journal entries reduced me to tears. The death of Melissa's beloved cat just days before her own tragic demise seemed to foreshadow the ending of a story she never intended to write. Thankfully, the poignant insight into Melissa's personal life offset the sadness I felt and provided a unique first-hand perspective of her life as an ordinary teenager. Those glimpses provided immeasurable value to law enforcement, my documentary team, and me personally as I learned about this young woman I am connected to on so many levels. I am forever grateful for the opportunity to experience Melissa's life through her own eyes. She painted a beautiful self-portrait in her diary of a kind, naive, innocent, and fun-loving young woman focused on a successful future.

Before my team left the police department that afternoon, Jay C. Rider stopped in to meet with us. He immediately noticed Melissa's journal.

"I see you have been doing some reading today," Rider commented.

"I've read it twice already," I responded.

He smiled knowingly. He understood all too well how difficult my task had been.

"Williams thinks her killer's name could be in that diary. What do you think?" I asked.

"I think..." he paused, "I think his name is on one of those pages, LaDonna. I really do. I think she knew the son of a bitch that killed her."

The emotional impact from reading her diary combined with Rider's words have help drive me on this exhausting and all-consuming quest to find justice for

Melissa Witt. My team and I have spent countless hours piecing together the clues and leads that flood our website and Facebook page, "Who Killed Missy Witt?". We are continually on the hunt for that one piece of information that connects a potential suspect back to Melissa's diary. We are forever haunted by the realization that the killer's name may have been innocently etched into the pages of that small 5 x 8 notebook by Melissa herself.

It's not farfetched to believe that Melissa's diary could someday lead to the resolution of her murder case. In 2011, the diary of a teenage girl murdered in Clayton County, Georgia led police to a suspect in her case more than a year after her death. On April 28, 2010, Candice Parchment, age 15, disappeared. Seven months later, in November of 2010, investigators found Parchment's remains underneath an old mattress in a wooded area near her home. Investigators had little information to go on until Parchment's mother, Caffian Hyatt, found her daughter's diary.

As Hyatt read the diary, she discovered the names of two teenage boys who had allegedly assaulted her daughter. Parchment had written about the gruesome details surrounding an attempted rape in an abandoned house at the hands of the two young men. According to the diary entry, Parchment had never reported the assault to the authorities because the boys had threatened her life.

Hyatt turned the diary over to the police in the hopes that it could solve her daughter's murder case. When investigators looked into the accusations in the diary, they discovered that one of the teenagers was already incarcerated in the Clayton County Jail. When interrogated, the young man allegedly confessed to strangling Parchment and hiding her body under a mattress. He was later found guilty of 12 charges, including murder and attempted rape in two separate incidents that led to the brutal murder of Candice Parchment.

The Parchment murder isn't the only case that has been solved from clues found in a victim's diary. On Sunday, June 8, 1986, Kathleen Lipscomb never arrived at the home of her estranged husband to pick up her children from their weekend visit with their father. This was out of character for Kathleen, and her friends and family immediately feared the worst. Unfortunately, their instincts proved to be right when her naked body was soon discovered in a field just outside of town. Lipscomb had been sexually assaulted and strangled.

Law enforcement immediately zeroed in on three different men: Lipscomb's husband, a coworker, and Kathleen's married lover. Despite law enforcement's best efforts, there was very little evidence to go on and the case grew cold. Desperate for answers, Lipscomb's family hired a private investigator. Almost immediately, the private investigator found several clues in Lipscomb's diary that ultimately led to the arrest of her killer – her estranged husband, William T. Lipscomb.

If the content of Parchment's and Lipscomb's diaries solved their murder cases, could the same thing happen in the Witt murder? Unlike Parchment and Lipscomb,

Melissa's diary, however, is no smoking gun. There is no finger pointing directly at any one potential suspect. Her diary, while true and authentic, provides only small glimpses into her life. In fact, large portions of her life never made it onto the pages of her journal for reasons only she will know. One can only assume that like most young women, including myself, Melissa was too busy to record information she felt was insignificant. I doubt that Melissa ever dreamed that every shred of information she had recorded would someday be needed as a clue in an investigation into her own murder.

Until her case is solved, law enforcement will always view the candid observations Melissa wrote about her life as a Westark Community College student as an important piece of evidence in the hunt to capture the man who murdered her. I will, however, always see Melissa's diary as sacred words that perfectly capture the crux of who she was: a pure innocent soul who deserves justice.

Chapter Eight
DEATH ROW

Four years after Melissa Witt's body was discovered in the Ozark National Forest, a rookie reporter named Marcus Blair came across significant information while working the police and fire beat for the *Times Record* in Fort Smith. As Blair sat in the newsroom thumbing through various newspapers, he stumbled upon front page news out of Houston, Texas.

A man named Larry Swearingen had been arrested for the murder of a young college student named Melissa Trotter. Swearingen was accused of strangling the 19-year-old to death and dumping her body in the Sam Houston National Forest.

Blair immediately noticed similarities between the murders of Melissa Trotter and Melissa Witt. Not only did both women have the same first name, they looked similar in physical appearance. Both young women had been abducted, strangled, and their bodies found in a national forest. But what struck Blair most was the eerie realization that Trotter and Witt were abducted four years apart to the week.

Knowing he had to act fast, Blair immediately contacted the Fort Smith Police Department and scheduled a meeting with Jay C. Rider, who at the time was the Captain of the Major Crimes Unit. By the time the meeting was over, investigators had their eyes set on a promising new lead in Melissa Witt's murder: Larry Ray Swearingen.

In 2021, I sat down with Marcus Blair inside the small Missouri church where he now serves as the pastor. That afternoon, Blair shared details of how his life and career intersected with the Melissa Witt murder case. "I had gone to work for the Fort Smith, Arkansas paper, the *Times Record*," Blair explained. "I was very young and wet behind the ears. I really don't think I knew quite what I was doing yet. The paper immediately put me on the police and fire beat which is known to be a trial by fire…. We received newspapers from all over the place and we kept an eye on the TV news. We made every attempt to stay aware of what was going on all over the place. I was looking through the Houston newspaper and there was front page news about the murder of a young woman named Melissa Trotter," said Blair. "I immediately thought, you know, wow, this girl looks like Melissa Witt. The more I read, the more I realized how similar the cases were to each other. The girls looked the same in appearance, clothing, college students, churchgoing, loved and respected in the community. The list went on and on."

As investigators dug into the new lead, it became clear that the similarities in the Witt and Trotter cases were too many and too striking for law enforcement to ignore. Like Blair, law enforcement discovered that both young women shared the same first name, appearance, and build, and both wore similar clothing at the time of their abductions. They were each missing similar personal effects. Both young women were found by hunters on national forest land about 50 miles from their abduction sites, and both had been strangled.

In Blair's *Times Record* article about his findings, he reported that "Capt. J.C. Rider of the Fort Smith Police Department, who has been heading the Witt investigation from its beginning, said the cases are mirror images of each other and could be the work of a serial killer."

"I've been waiting for a guy like this to come along since the case began," Rider told me during our meeting. "I've never seen two cases this similar, but I've also run into more coincidences in this case than any other. But the coincidence is almost unbelievable."

The article goes on to say that "Rider has been placing one phone call after another since receiving the information, hoping to find some record of Swearingen in Fort Smith.

"So far, no traffic citations, offense reports, accident reports or pawn slips have yielded results. But Rider thinks the best hope of linking Swearingen to Fort Smith will come from his employment records.

"Montgomery County investigators have formed a timeline which tracks Swearingen's movements up to two years ago. Police have learned he was a journeyman electrician who traveled through the Southeast, along the east coast and as far north as New England in search of work. Rider thinks local electricians might have records of Swearingen's possible employment in Fort Smith."

What Detective Rider discovered next would set the Witt case on fire. Just days before the Witt murder Larry Swearingen had been in Arkansas visiting his grandparents in Clinton. While there, Swearingen purchased a part for his car. Detective Rider drove to Clinton and tracked down a copy of the receipt. The receipt was not enough to tie Swearingen, even circumstantially, to Witt's murder. However, the receipt, the similarities between the Trotter and Witt murders, and proof of Swearingen's presence in Arkansas just days before Witt's death, combined with another strange turn of events did, according to Rider, make Swearingen a suspect."

"I believe it was after I retired from the Fort Smith Police Department," Rider later told me. "I became the Chief of Police in Barling, Arkansas, just outside of Fort Smith. One day I received a call from the Texas Attorney General's office. They shared with me that in a routine cell check on death row, guards found paperwork in Swearingen's own handwriting under his mattress that listed out my name, Melissa Witt's name, and the date December 1, 1994. It was definitely a strange twist in the case. We can't rule Swearingen out. In fact, he's the top suspect in Melissa's murder. There are just too many things lining up against him."

Melissa Aline Trotter, a 19-year-old outgoing college student, went missing on December 8, 1998 in Willis, Texas. Trotter was last seen alive at the student center at Lone Star College Montgomery Campus. Swearingen, at the time, was a 27-year-old married man with a long history of problems with the law. According to authorities, Larry Swearingen was the last person seen with Trotter on the day she went missing.

Three days after Trotter's disappearance, Swearingen, driving a stolen red pick-up truck, was arrested for outstanding traffic warrants. While detained, Swearingen was questioned about Trotter's disappearance. He told investigators that he "didn't even know the girl existed." His statement would be the first of dozens of lies Swearingen would tell authorities over the course of the Trotter case.

Twenty-five days after her disappearance, on January 2, 1999, hunters found the body of Melissa Trotter in a secluded location in the Sam Houston National Forest. She was partially clothed and had been strangled with a leg segment cut from a pair of pantyhose.

Investigators quickly closed in on Swearingen. When a search of the stolen truck he had been driving revealed strands of hair belonging to Trotter, Swearingen suddenly changed his story. Now he admitted that he not only knew Trotter, but she had been in his truck multiple times. "We were dating. Friends with benefits. We went out and had a good time."

Later, while in the county jail awaiting trial, Swearingen gave his cellmate, Ronnie Coleman, a letter that appeared to be written in Spanish and asked Coleman to copy it onto another piece of paper because, he claimed, his grandmother had difficulty reading his handwriting. Coleman copied the letter as Swearingen asked.

Once Coleman completed the task, Swearingen sent the letter to his mother. He told her that he had received the letter in jail. Believing the lie, Swearingen's mother and stepfather took it to investigators. The letter contained an account of Trotter's murder by someone alleging to have personal knowledge of the heinous crime. A professional translator was asked to review the letter and determined it was written with an English grammatical structure as though someone had simply translated English words directly from a Spanish dictionary.

That letter proved to be damning. It contained information about Trotter's murder that only the killer could know: "I saw everything that happened to Melissa… we talked about sex when she said she had to go home. He hit her in the left eye, and she fell to the floor of her car. He took her to the woods and began to choke her with his hands at first, then he jerked her to the bushes. He cut her throat to make sure she was dead. Her shoe came off when he jerked her into the bushes. To make sure you know I am telling the truth, she was murdered wearing red panties when R.D. murdered her." The letter was signed "Robin."

In Swearingen's cell, authorities discovered a handwritten list of Spanish-to-English word translations that included dozens of the words and phrases from the letter in question. A handwriting analyst determined that

Swearingen had written the Spanish-to-English translation. Fingerprints from both Coleman and Swearingen were also found on the letter sent to Larry Swearingen's mother. When confronted with all of the evidence, Swearingen was forced to admit he had orchestrated the writing of the bizarre confession. He claimed he was terrified of being executed so he took information gleaned from autopsy reports and photos to piece together the strange story. This would not be the last time Swearingen would try to fool investigators.

In 2017, while awaiting execution for Trotter's murder, Swearingen conspired with Houston's "Tourniquet Killer," Anthony Allen Shore. Swearingen convinced Shore to claim responsibility for the murder of Melissa Trotter. Montgomery County Texas District Attorney Brett Ligon was quoted by The Courier as saying, "I am not surprised in the least that Swearingen would have attempted this scheme to avoid his overdue date with justice.... As the appellate courts have stressed, there is a mountain of evidence supporting the conviction of Mr. Swearingen."

That *mountain of evidence* against Swearingen was enormous. Among them, records showed that a cell tower "pinged" Swearingen's phone near where Melissa Trotter's body was found and fibers from his stolen truck were discovered on her coat. The match of the murder weapon (pantyhose) was also found at his residence.

At trial, his cell mate, Bill Kory, testified that Swearingen told him, "Fuck yeah, I killed her. I'm just trying to beat the death penalty." And in July 2000, based on the evidence presented, Larry Ray Swearingen was convicted by a jury of his peers of capital murder. He was sentenced to death for killing Trotter during the course of committing or attempting to commit aggravated sexual assault.

To better understand this monster, I spent hundreds of hours sorting through news articles and interviewing dozens of people in Texas. Almost immediately, a common theme emerged. Larry Ray Swearingen had a long history of violent acts against women.

One of the first things I discovered about Swearingen particularly disturbed me. It turns out he was already under indictment for the kidnapping and sexual assault of his former fiancé when he kidnapped, raped, and murdered Melissa Trotter. But that's not all. In 1992, Swearingen was convicted of shooting at and then kidnapping his wife and sexually assaulting her at a remote location in the woods off Airport Road in Montgomery County, Texas. According to testimony during the punishment phase of his trial, a former neighbor testified that Swearingen broke into her house, rummaged through her lingerie, and cut off the legs of a pair of pantyhose. One can only assume his intent was malicious.

In 1994, the same year that Melissa Witt was murdered, Swearingen tied up, gagged, and sexually assaulted a young female after forcing her to don pantyhose from which the crotch had been removed.

In 1997, Swearingen choked his nine-month-pregnant wife nearly to the point of unconsciousness after accusing her of being unfaithful. Then, in August 1998, he handcuffed, choked, and sexually assaulted his former fiancé. One month later, in September 1998, Swearingen again abducted his former fiancé at gunpoint and forced her to drive to a remote dirt road in the Sam Houston National Forest before releasing her.

It is no surprise to me that a jury found Swearingen guilty of capital murder. They also found there was a probability he would commit further criminal acts of violence that would constitute a continuing threat to society. There is no doubt that Larry Swearingen was an incredibly dangerous man.

Next, I reached out to Swearingen's friends, relatives, and former wives. At the time, Swearingen was on death row awaiting execution by the State of Texas. Most people, especially his ex-wives, were fearful to speak out against him. The information they shared with me in confidence was absolutely frightening. They shared stories of rape, strangulation, and horrific violence at the hands of Swearingen. His victims lived in absolute fear—each haunted by the memories of their terrible encounters.

During the interview process, I asked each woman the same question. Do you think it's possible that Larry Swearingen killed Melissa Witt? Without hesitation each and every woman answered my question the exact same way: "Yes, I think Larry killed Melissa Witt." One woman went further to say, "Larry was in Kansas working on a job site there just weeks before Witt was killed. I know for a fact Larry left that job and went on to Arkansas to see his grandparents. I've always thought he killed the Witt girl. I will go to my grave believing that he did it."

After the compelling statements made about Swearingen, I knew it was time to ask the death row inmate some questions myself. I spent a week formulating my thoughts before typing out a letter to him.

Seven days after I mailed my letter, I received a response from the Polunsky Unit in Livingston, Texas. I hastily ripped open the envelope to discover a neatly typed, one paragraph response from Swearingen:

> Dear LaDonna, received your letter dated March 27, 2017, this evening and wanted to reply. Understand your meaning well with your project, truly do, but I cannot participate in anything without prior approval of counsel. It's not just you, anyone that conducts interviews with me is pre-approved by counsel. Get with counsel and have everything approved, otherwise I'm truly sorry [I'm] just not able to participate. In case the contact information has been lost, please find counsel's information below. Take care and God bless.
>
> Sincerely, Larry Swearingen.

I was perplexed by his response. At that point, I had personally made over a dozen attempts to contact Swearingen's counsel. Each call, email, fax, and letter was ignored. Frustrated, I decided to write to Swearingen again. This decision proved to be pivotal in setting the tone for my relationship with the convicted murderer. On Tuesday, April 11, 2017, I mailed a handwritten letter to Swearingen. It contained only five words: "Did you kill Melissa Witt?"

A month later, I received a cryptic response postmarked from Conroe, Texas. This letter was not mailed from a prison and it did not include a return address. The contents of the note were short and to the point. The anonymous author wrote: "Larry Swearingen did not kill Melissa Witt. Leave Larry alone. He knows what you are up to. Go to hell, bitch!"

I quickly penned my next letter to Swearingen. "Write to me yourself. I am not interested in anonymous letters sent on your behalf, Mr. Swearingen. You have been convicted and sentenced to death for a murder that is almost identical to a murder in Arkansas. So my question is simple. Did you kill Melissa Witt? I know you were in Arkansas within days of her death, Larry. Were you ever in Fort Smith? Did you meet Melissa? If you didn't kill her, this should be an easy answer to provide. What's your alibi for December 1, 1994? I look forward to your response."

Swearingen sent a strong message in response to my pointed questions. Instead of a letter, he countered with an official cease and desist sent by his attorney. Interestingly, my calls and emails to his attorney on this matter went unanswered. Over the next year and a half, I received multiple anonymous letters postmarked from Conroe, Texas. It's evident the communication was orchestrated by the death row inmate. I always responded to the anonymous correspondence the same way. I sent handwritten notes directly to Swearingen, pressing him for answers. Like clockwork, he would, in return, serve me with a cease and desist.

Tiring of the chess game, I turned to social media for help. At that time, my Facebook page, "Who Killed Missy Witt," had grown to well over 7,000 followers. I posted a public plea for information about the convicted murderer and within hours my inbox was bursting with over eighty messages. Former drinking buddies, girlfriends, death row guards, and distant family members shared accusations of terrible deeds committed by Swearingen. Their words dripped with righteous fury as they recounted his alleged crimes ranging from lying and theft to rape and assault.

The next day, I received two interesting emails. The first came from a source in law enforcement out of Montgomery County who wishes to remain anonymous. They shared with me details about a receipt allegedly found in the stolen truck that Swearingen was driving when he was arrested on outstanding traffic warrants. According to my source, the receipt was from a store in Fort Smith, Arkansas and was dated around the time of Melissa Witt's abduction and murder. The source went on to say that Texas officials believed that Larry was probably tied to the Witt murder. However, they decided before his trial that if Larry received the death penalty they would not pursue the murder in Arkansas. Stunned, I began a phone and email campaign asking officials in Montgomery County,

Texas about the receipt. Unfortunately, the receipt, if it exists, was somehow lost.

The second email I received was from a German woman named Wiebke Schlue Swearingen. Wiebke started off as a pen pal of Swearingen's and eventually became his best friend and fiercest advocate. Later, she also became his wife.

Wiebke's email to me that afternoon was bitter and accusatory. She insulted my efforts to connect Swearingen to Melissa Witt's murder. But her email also confirmed important information. According to Wiebke, Swearingen had been working in Kansas and Arkansas in late 1994. In my response to Wiebke, I asked her to provide Swearingen's alibi for December 1. If he's innocent, I reasoned, Swearingen would be willing to help investigators rule him out as a suspect in Witt's murder. It turns out my request offended Wiebke and it served as fuel for a series of heated emails between us that same afternoon. Her last communication stated, "Larry is watching you on the Internet. You won't get away with accusing him of the Witt murder." The truth is that I have never accused Larry Swearingen of killing Melissa Witt. I have, however, pursued answers to what happened on that cold December evening in 1994.

Swearingen worked for years to cast doubt on the evidence used to convict him in the Trotter murder. He was fortunate to be represented by a team of passionate attorneys, including the Innocence Project. Their hard work gifted Swearingen with five separate stays of execution. As his final date of execution approached, I anxiously began to call and email authorities in Texas, hoping to arrange an interview between Swearingen and officials investigating the Witt murder. Luckily, shortly before his scheduled August 21, 2019 execution, Texas officials contacted authorities in Arkansas to set up an interview with Swearingen.

Jay C. Rider, Chris Boyd, and Detective Brad Marion drove to Texas for the death row interrogation. Upon their arrival, they were ushered into a room where they finally, after years of waiting, met Larry Ray Swearingen face-to-face.

"We go in, sit down, and prepare for the meeting. Guards bring Larry back and he's pleasant. He's smiling and in good spirits," Rider tells me on a phone call after his return from Texas. "Larry sits down, looks at us and asks, 'What are you guys here for?' Chris Boyd tells him, you know, we are detectives from Fort Smith, Arkansas."

What happened next baffled investigators. Without warning, Swearingen rose from his seat and nonchalantly said, "That's it. This interview is over. I don't want to talk to you guys. I want to go back to my cell." His refusal to talk was a devastating blow to the Witt case. Eight short weeks later, the 48-year-old convicted rapist and murderer received a lethal injection at the state penitentiary in Huntsville, Texas. The man who maintained his innocence in the murder of Melissa Trotter and evaded questioning in the murder of Melissa Witt for over two decades was pronounced dead at 6:47pm, twelve minutes after he was given a lethal dose of pentobarbital.

A few weeks after Swearingen's execution, my husband sent me this text message: "USPS delivered a large envelope to the house, it's pretty thick. It's addressed to you and it's postmarked from Texas." Curious, I drove home as soon as I could to open the package. Inside, I discovered various 8x10 color photos of Larry Swearingen taken shortly after his execution. The package also contained a 20-page letter allegedly sent by one of Swearingen's relatives. It accused me of assisting the State of Texas in murdering Larry Swearingen. The hateful diatribe also included threats against my life.

The next day, I opened my Facebook messenger and discovered dozens of ugly messages from people I had never met. In them, I am blamed for Swearingen's execution and many of them threatened violence against my family. Overwhelmed with shock and panic, I notified local authorities. It's been almost two years since Swearingen's execution and, believe it or not, I continue to receive startling messages like those.

Recently, I discovered a book published about Swearingen. I purchased a copy and was astonished to read the following passage: "In her insatiable anger, she created at least three different pages on facebook.com against Larry. One of them is the ham-fisted attempt to connect Larry with the unsolved murder of Melissa 'Missy' Witt, because Ms. Witt had characteristics similar to Melissa Trotter."

Shockingly, the author suggests that the person behind the Melissa Witt Facebook page is a resident of Texas who once engaged in a brief sexual relationship with Larry Swearingen in the 1990s. To my knowledge, I am the only person connected to a Facebook page that seeks justice for Melissa Witt and questions Larry Swearingen's possible involvement in her murder. I've never lived in Texas and I most certainly never had a relationship with Larry Ray Swearingen. The false statements in the book, just like the Facebook messages and the mysterious package sent to my home, are nothing more than lame attempts to intimidate and undermine me as I investigate Swearingen's possible involvement in Melissa's death.

That same author also claimed that Swearingen was working at a Sears store in Kansas at the time of Witt's murder, and that employment records would show he was nowhere near Fort Smith on December 1, 1994. If that information proves to be accurate, it's possible that Larry Swearingen will be ruled out as a suspect in this case once and for all. Until that day comes, however, Larry Swearingen will remain a top suspect in the murder of Melissa Ann Witt.

Chapter Nine
CHURCH CAMP

Over the years, my team has received dozens of tips about a man with deep ties to Ozark, Arkansas. Dark rumors about his involvement in Melissa's murder have swelled since 1998 when law enforcement released his name as part of the Witt investigation.

Travis Dale Crouch officially became a person of interest in Melissa's murder shortly after he was sentenced to 64 years in prison for the sexual assault of a 20-year-old woman from Broomfield, Colorado in July 1997.

According to police records, Crouch was panhandling at a Boulder, Colorado shopping mall when he started talking to a young woman. The situation quickly escalated to violence and Crouch kidnapped the frightened woman in her own car and drove her to a remote mountaintop. There, Crouch brutally sexually assaulted his helpless victim. After the attack, the young woman escaped with her life when Crouch passed out in her car from a drug-induced stupor. Crouch was arrested a short time later near the same area where the rape had taken place.

In 1999, Marcus Blair, the reporter with the Southwest Times Record who wrote the breakout story about Larry Swearingen and the similarities between the Melissa Trotter murder in Texas and the murder of Melissa Witt, also wrote about Travis Crouch:

> Crouch was a carpenter at a church camp north of Ozark where Witt's body was found, and police say he was seen driving a bronze Chevrolet Caprice near Bowling World at the time of Witt's disappearance. "Hair, fiber and stain samples taken from the car in March 1998 have been sent to the FBI for evaluation, but tests have not been completed," Rider said. Police said Crouch grew up in the Franklin County area where Witt's body was found and often hunted there. Because Witt's body was found during deer season in such a remote area, police believed only a hunter familiar with the area could have dumped the body without being caught.

The church camp Blair mentions in the news article is located just a few miles down the road from where Melissa's body was found on Forest Service Road 1551. The Baptist Vista Church Camp, is located on Shores Lake Road just off of Highway 23 in Ozark, Arkansas. Open to visitors during the summer, in December 1994, when Melissa Witt was kidnapped, the camp was closed to the public as usual.

According to law enforcement, Travis Crouch was intimately familiar with the church camp and surrounding area. As it turns out, his father and stepmother had worked as the Baptist Vista Camp groundskeepers. Crouch spent his formative years in that lonely yet beautiful stretch of the Ozark National Forest just off of Lake Shores Road. Later, as a rebellious teenager and young adult, Crouch, using the nicknames "Tramp" and "Skull," spread his wings and traveled across the United States to places such as New Orleans, Phoenix, Flagstaff, Myrtle Beach, Charlotte, and Las Vegas. While he sometimes traveled alone, Crouch was also known to ride with some of the most dangerous motorcycle gangs in the United States. He often managed to find trouble on his travels, and in October of 1994, after serving time in Minneapolis for stabbing a man, Crouch, barefoot and with only the clothes he had on his back, hitchhiked back to his hometown of Ozark.

According to Jay C. Rider, Travis Crouch never provided an alibi for his whereabouts on December 1, 1994. "We have witnesses that place him in Ozark, Arkansas at least through mid-December 1994," Rider said. "Records show that Crouch was arrested and put in jail on January 1, 1995 in New Orleans, Louisiana. But his whereabouts up until that time remain unknown."

As information about Travis Crouch steadily poured into my inbox, I went to work researching this mysterious and menacing character. I quickly stumbled upon a news article about Crouch's conviction for the rape in Boulder, Colorado:

> A convicted rapist was sentenced to 64 years in prison Monday after a profanity-laced outburst that got him ejected from the courtroom. 'To hell with you,' the 31-year old Travis Dale Crouch shared as District Court Judge Morris Sandstead ordered him removed.... Just prior to handing down the sentence, Sandstead called Crouch a 'sexual predator and a danger to others.... No sentence that can be imposed by this court can make the defendant understand the depth of his criminality,' Sandstead said.

I picked up the phone to call Detective Troy Williams. "Would it be okay for me to come by this afternoon and read the files on Travis Crouch?" I asked. Williams agreed. Within hours, I was sitting at a table across from Detective Williams reading a comprehensive report about the investigation into Travis Dale Crouch. After reading through the volumes of information, it was obvious that he was a violent career criminal. But was he responsible for the kidnapping and murder of Melissa? I can't be sure. And neither is law enforcement.

I left the Fort Smith Police Department that afternoon determined to find solid answers about Travis Crouch. I decided the best approach would be to once again harness the power of social media. I posted the information I'd found in the newspaper articles from the late 1990s about Crouch on my Facebook page, "Who Killed Missy Witt?" Within hours, I was contacted by people all across the United States. Stories of rape, violent assaults, robbery, arson, and stabbings filled my inbox.

One account, written by a man who proclaimed to be a reformed ex-member of a violent motorcycle gang, caught my attention. He alleged he was once a close friend of Travis Crouch's and has reason to believe that he could be responsible for Melissa's murder. He wrote:

> I know it may be hard to believe but I am a different man now than I was when Skull and I ran together. I did some bad things myself, but you need to understand that Skull was a different kind of bad. Life means nothing to Skull. I've watched him stab a man and I've heard him talk endlessly about women he has raped. I think you might also be interested in the fact that Skull married a gal named Melissa. That relationship ended badly not too long before he headed to Arkansas and Skull wasn't one bit too happy about it either.

The author of the next message I received alleged that Crouch physically and emotionally abused his wife. "Travis also forced his wife to watch on as he sexually assaulted women that he lured back to their apartment." The last sentence of the message sent chills down my spine: "I believe that Crouch's old lady was lucky to make it out of that relationship alive. I believe there were others that were not so lucky and I believe Melissa Witt was one of them."

After reading those horrific accusations, I was determined to find Crouch's ex-wife in hopes of interviewing her for my documentary. After months of searching, I finally located the former Mrs. Travis Crouch. During our first phone call, she shared with me that she feared for her life and begged me to never disclose her full name or location. "I am shocked you found me," she said. "If you can find me, I fear that once Travis is out of prison, he can find me too. Please never give out my personal information. You have to understand that Travis Crouch is a very, very dangerous man. If he ever finds me, I have no doubt that he will kill me."

It was disturbing to hear Crouch's ex-wife describe how she had not only witnessed but also survived his violent outbursts of utter rage. She sobbed as she shared painful details of abuse that had forever changed her life. "The abuse began almost immediately after our wedding day and continued until the day I escaped with my life. You have to understand that everything Travis did was extreme," she said. "Domestic violence, drug use, crime— all of it was extreme, excessive, and horrifically violent."

Equally disturbing, in my opinion, is the fact that both she and Witt shared the same first name. That detail was not lost on her either. "I can't get past the fact that my name is also Melissa and that we looked so much alike back then," she confided to me one afternoon. "You don't think he was angry with me over our divorce and ended up killing Melissa Witt because of it, do you? I have always worried that somehow the end of our relationship created a rage in him that caused him to do something horrific to that poor girl."

"I don't think that is a burden you should carry," I responded. "If he is responsible for the murder of Melissa Witt, that's solely on Travis. Nothing you said or did, including the divorce, justifies violence of any kind. The monster that killed Melissa Witt on Thursday, December 1, 1994 is the only one to blame. Nobody else. Only him."

A few days after talking with Crouch's frightened ex-wife for the first time, I decided it was time to write to him in the Arkansas Valley Correctional Facility in Colorado. Travis Crouch wasn't the first inmate I had written to over the course of my investigation into the Witt case, and I assumed, like the others, he would respond to my letter within a few weeks. But I was wrong. When six months passed with no reply, I wrote another letter. Another four months passed and still no response. Why wasn't Crouch responding to my letters? Frustrated, I wrote another letter. And then another. This pattern continued for the next five years. I would write to Crouch, wait months for a response, and when none came, I would write again. At one point, I even resorted to calling the correctional facility to confirm that Travis Dale Crouch, inmate #97668, was in fact receiving my correspondence. The facility director assured me that my letters had been delivered: "I suspect he simply doesn't want to communicate with you, Ms.

Humphrey." I refused to give up. I answered Crouch's deafening silence with steely determination. I kept writing him letters.

A few months after sending one such letter, I was eating lunch with a dear friend and fellow true crime advocate, and she casually mentioned an email service she was using to correspond with an inmate in Colorado. "The service is easy to use," she said. "If you have the inmate's DOC number, just create an account and you can send an email for a small fee. The facility will print the email and deliver it to the inmate within 24 hours." She suggested I try to contact Travis Crouch using the email service. Later that evening, I took her advice and signed up. In my email, I asked Crouch to please consider answering my correspondence. "After all," I wrote, "if you have nothing to hide in the Witt case, I could actually help you get your name cleared." Three weeks later as I was in the middle of cooking dinner for my family, my husband casually asked, "Did you happen to look through the mail when you got home from work today?"

"No, I haven't looked at it yet. Anything good?" I responded.

"Oh… maybe," he chuckled. "You received a letter from Travis Crouch."

I stared at my husband in disbelief as he handed me the letter. After five long years my persistence had paid off. Travis Dale Crouch had finally responded to me. I sat down at the kitchen table and carefully opened the thick envelope. It took almost an hour to read through the six pages of tiny print that Travis Crouch had scrawled from inside his Colorado prison cell. To my surprise, the letter contained blunt and sometimes humorous details about his life behind bars and the experiences that led him there. Crouch also included an outright denial of any involvement in Melissa Witt's murder. "I didn't kill that girl," Crouch wrote. "And I would appreciate it greatly if you would stop asking me about it. I did not kill Melissa Witt. You need to spend your time finding out who killed her because it ain't me, LaDonna Humphrey. It ain't me."

Since that first letter almost a year ago, Crouch and I have continued to correspond with each other. However, until law enforcement either rules Crouch out as a suspect or charges him with Melissa's murder, I will not disclose the details of our correspondence to the public. But what I will share is this: Crouch continues to maintain his innocence in Melissa's murder. "I have said it before and I will say it again," Crouch wrote in his most recent letter. "I did not kill Melissa Witt. It was not me."

⌘

One day, my team and I visited the Baptist Vista Church Camp. As I stood at the entrance, thoughts of Travis Crouch, his letters, and the rumors of his involvement in Melissa's murder weighed heavily on my mind. I prepared myself for the task ahead. My team and I were on location to test out a theory that had been shared with us at least a dozen times. Multiple people from across the United

States sent in tips describing a scenario where Melissa Witt was held against her will in one of the cabins at the church camp. One tip provided a detailed description of how "Melissa escaped from the cabin, barefoot, and ran from her captor until he finally caught up with her at the location where her body was found."

My team and I carefully reexamined the crime scene photos as well as Melissa's autopsy report. Our goal was to better understand the condition of Melissa's feet—particularly the bottoms of her feet. Once we were confident with our understanding of the facts, it was time to test out the theory ourselves. What would happen if we ran the distance barefoot from the church camp to the logging road where Melissa's body was discovered?

The area where Melissa Witt's body was found can only be accessed from the Baptist Vista Church Camp in two ways: directly from Lake Shores Road or indirectly by walking through the forest. As we prepared to access the logging road indirectly through a path in the forest, we quickly determined it would have been almost impossible for Melissa to get very far using this route. The landscape of the forest floor is a carpet of constantly changing inclines, jagged rocks, fallen trees, and overgrown thorny bushes. If Melissa had somehow chosen this way to escape, her body would have shown signs of trauma such as cuts, bruises, scratches, and other injuries. There were no indicators of these types of wounds in the autopsy report.

With the forest route now ruled out, our team began setting up our gear near the entrance of the Baptist Vista Church Camp. After removing my shoes and socks, I stood awkwardly on the dusty gravel road. I shifted back and forth as small jagged rocks nipped at the soles of my feet. I braced myself to run. In the distance, a team member yelled "Go!" and I took off.

The gravel road, made up of a mixture of small rocks and red dirt, required much more effort than regular, soft ground. I winced as hundreds of tiny rocks tore at my feet, sending shooting pains through my feet and legs. Tears ran down my face as I pictured a terrified Melissa running this same road in an attempt to save her life. As I ran, I could hear the sound of shoe heels skidding on the ground behind me as my captor closed in. My heart was racing. He was getting closer. I tried to run faster, but my efforts were useless. The man pursuing me was stronger and quicker. I screamed as he tackled me to the ground. It was over. I sat on the side of the gravel road in defeat. I had run less than half a mile down the lonely, dusty road before I was caught. I walked back to the entrance of the church camp where my team greeted me with a first-aid kit filled with bandages, athletic tape, and Tylenol. I was bruised and sore but, fortunately, my injuries were not serious.

We left the Ozark National Forest convinced that while it was possible Melissa could have escaped her captor and ran barefoot down Lake Shores Road, it was very unlikely that this scenario took place. Even after Melissa's fight or flight response kicked in, she would have been physically limited by how fast her body could actually run on that gravel road. I also acknowledge that our efforts, while well-intentioned, were far from scientific. In reality, we knew it was impossible for our team to recreate a true life-and-death situation. But we felt it was important for us to experience this together as a team. And while our efforts did not lead to a conclusive answer, our time on Lake Shores Road was far from wasted. We were reminded that the world is sometimes a dangerous place and our personal control can be ripped away from us in an instant. Experiencing what could have happened to Melissa Witt in the Ozark National Forest that afternoon cemented in our hearts and minds the importance of our work. We had become the voice for Melissa and a force that will not stop until justice finds its way to the man who took her life. And justice is coming. I can feel it.

Chapter Ten
THE SKETCH

One morning as I sat at my desk flipping through a large stack of newspaper articles written about Melissa's abduction and murder, a story published by the Southwest Times Record on May 17, 1995 caught my eye: "Police ask for help finding Witt witness." The story, a plea to the public to help identify this man, was compelling. Shocked, I picked up the phone to call Detective Williams. "A witness in the Witt case?" I asked. "What the hell? Can you meet?" Williams agreed and, within minutes, I was on my way to the Fort Smith Police Department.

After the hour-long trek from Northwest Arkansas, I arrived at the police station and took the elevator up to the detective division. Detective Williams greeted me in the lobby. My mind was on overdrive as we walked down the hallway to his office. "This man," I said as I pointed to the article I was holding, "was seen changing clothes near the site where Melissa's body was found. According to the author, he is not considered a suspect but police wanted to bring him in for questioning." I took off my coat, placed the newspaper clipping on his desk, and tapped it for effect.

"Well, you are certainly on fire today," Williams laughed.

"Sorry about that," I muttered before immediately shrugging off his comment to tap on the article again. "A witness saw this man and said he didn't appear to have any hunting equipment. He looked out of place. And he was changing clothes!" I tapped the paper a third time. "This has to be important, don't you think? Do you know if this man was ever questioned?"

"I'll be honest. I just don't know," Williams said. "We'll need to check the files. You have to remember that I am very new to this case and there is an overwhelming amount of information to read through. We'll have to do some research."

"Okay... let's research it. Let's do it now. Right now. I can help," I pleaded. "I feel strongly that this could be important. And it would ease my mind to know who this guy is and if he was ruled out as someone of interest in Witt's murder."

Detective Williams leaned back in his chair, never breaking eye contact with me, and said, "Your passion is contagious, Humphrey," and he picked up the phone.

"Who are you calling?" I asked.

Detective Williams smiled as he switched the call to speakerphone. As the shrill "ring, ring, ring" of the phone danced through the cubicle, I leaned in closer and continued my story in a loud whisper, "The unidentified man was seen changing clothes next to a dark gray or black newer model car. The car had what appeared to be a racing stripe or decal on the passenger side rear quarter panel that was possibly purple and blue. The car also had a clothes rack hanging in the back seat, a spoiler on the trunk, and what appeared to be a college parking permit sticker. This guy…" I was cut off in mid-sentence when the phone stopped ringing.

A deep voice boomed on the other end. "Detective Troy Williams! How the hell are you?"

Williams and I made eye contact again. Feigning disbelief, I mouthed the words, "You called Jay C.?" Williams smiled, winked, and leaned back in his chair.

"Humphrey's here," Williams laughed.

Rider's laugh echoed over the speaker. "Well, of course she is," Rider joked. "I think she plans to move in over there! You should give her a desk!"

I rolled my eyes as Williams looked over his shoulder and said, "Did I mention you are on speakerphone?"

"Hey there," I sang out. But before Rider could respond, I launched into a series of questions about the man seen at the dumpsite.

Rider listened intently as I read the article out loud. "This says he was described as 20-30 years of age, 5 feet 11 inches tall, and weighing about 180 pounds with curly strawberry blond hair. He possibly had a beard."

"I hate to disappoint you, but the truth is we never did find that guy," Rider said. "And it certainly wasn't for a lack of trying."

"It seemed so promising..." I said as my voice trailed off.

Rider, sensing my disappointment, quickly interjected. "I tell you what. It just so happens that I'm close by. So why don't I come by the station after lunch? We can talk through this and go over some other things in the case."

"That sounds great," Williams said.

"Sounds good," I replied.

"I'll meet you both at the Police Department in two hours," Rider promised. "See you soon."

The phone went dead.

Williams looked at me and said, "I've got some paperwork to do, but you are welcome to stay until Rider gets here."

"No thanks," I said as I smiled and grabbed my coat. "There's something I need to do. But I'll be back."

"Suit yourself," said Williams. "See you in a few hours."

Outside the police station, I pulled out my iPhone, opened the Google Maps app, typed in the words "Woodlawn Memorial Park," and took a deep breath. It was time to go and pay my respects to Melissa Witt.

Twenty minutes later, I pulled into the cemetery on State Line Road. The expansive and tranquil landscape at Woodlawn Memorial Park is a peaceful, comforting, and picturesque backdrop for families to lay their loved ones to rest. "This is the perfect place," I thought to myself.

Raindrops gently began to fall as I parked my car. I turned off the engine and was immediately overcome with emotion. My stomach was in knots. "Is it okay that I am here?" I thought to myself as I fumbled to secure two neatly bundled packages of pink roses sitting in my passenger seat. "I hope that I am not intruding."

I shakily opened my car door and stepped onto the gravel road that lined the cemetery. The temperature had dropped significantly. I shivered from the bitter chill in the air. I reached into my coat pocket for my gloves before pulling out the crude map drawn to guide me in finding Melissa's final resting place in the large cemetery.

I looked up from the map and started across the damp grass. After just a few minutes, I found myself standing directly in front of a simple plaque with the words "Melissa Ann Witt. 1975-1995." My heart sank. "I'm sorry," I whispered. "I'm so very sorry."

I stood there for several minutes before leaning down to place the bouquets. One for Melissa. The other for Mary Ann Witt. "I really don't know why I am here," I said out loud and turned to leave. But my heart was heavy and I remained frozen in place. I could not walk away. Instead, I stood alone in the cemetery, sharing sacred and sincere thoughts and feelings with a girl I never knew.

The rain stopped as I slowly made my way back to the car. I started the engine just as the sun peaked out from behind the clouds. I smiled. As I drove away, a new sense of determination settled over me. "Justice," I whispered. "Justice for Melissa Witt."

I arrived back at the Fort Smith Police Department just as Rider was pulling into the parking lot. After exchanging a few pleasantries and hugs, Rider pointed toward the glass doors of the police department and I followed him inside.

Upstairs, Rider and I sat down with Detective Williams and discussed the newspaper article at length. "Jay C.," I said, "in this article, you gave a description of the car. You said it was similar to that of a Chevrolet Monte Carlo and that it was believed to have Arkansas license plates." I paused and then said, "The article also says this man was seen in that location just days after Melissa disappeared. Could he have been revisiting the crime scene?" I asked.

"It's possible," Rider answered. "But we just don't know."

Williams crossed his arms and said, "Well, we could release the information about this guy on social media. Maybe we would get lucky and someone would recognize him after all these years."

"We could," Rider said matter-of-factly, "but that composite sketch isn't the best quality. Have you taken a good look at it? It's way too generic. Don't get me wrong, I am not opposed to trying, but this is a long shot."

"I think the details about the man's hair and the details about the car might stand out to someone," I reasoned. "I agree with Williams. Let's put it out on social media and see what happens."

"Let's give it a try," Rider agreed. "It can't hurt anything."

"I can prepare something to post on the Facebook page as early as tomorrow," I assured them. "But first, I have one more question."

"Shoot," Rider said.

"Can I have the names of the hunters that saw this guy changing clothes?" I asked. "I would like to try and track them down and interview them."

Rider and Williams looked at each other knowingly.

Williams nodded his head in agreement. "Yes, okay. Go ahead."

After writing down the information I requested, Williams looked up at me and laughed as he said, "Here you go, Humphrey. Go get 'em!"

Rider smiled.

The next day I spent an hour crafting a social media post describing the man in question. I attached a copy of the composite sketch along with a portion of the May 1995 newspaper article and clicked the "share" button on Facebook. "Here we go," I thought. "Let's see what happens."

Within minutes, people were reading, liking, and sharing the post. My hope soared. I sent Williams a text. I typed the words "The Facebook post is gaining traction," and hit send.

"Fingers crossed," he responded.

While I waited on results from the Facebook post, I pulled out the names of the witnesses who reported seeing the man at the dumpsite. A quick Google search provided a possible lead. I called the number: "Hi, um, my name is LaDonna Humphrey and I am a journalist working on the 1995 abduction of a young girl named Melissa Witt from Fort Smith," I said. "I think… I hope I've reached the right number." I finished the message with additional details from the newspaper article and asked for a return call.

I stood up from my desk and paced back and forth. "There has to be more I can do to find this guy. But what?" I thought.

My phone rang. A familiar number flashed across my Caller ID. The man I left a message for just minutes earlier was already calling me back!

"Hello?" I answered excitedly.

"Is this LaDonna Humphrey?" he asked.

"Hi, yes it is," I responded. "Thank you so much for calling me back!"

"Sure, of course. What questions do you have for me?" the man asked. "I'm happy to help. I do remember that day and what I saw on that logging road."

I held the phone in my hand as I danced across the room to my desk. "Let's start from the beginning," I said.

Our call ended forty-five minutes later. I was now convinced that the young man changing clothes deep in the Ozark National Forest that December day was somehow connected to the murder of Melissa Witt.

"Let's see if anyone has recognized him," I said to myself as I logged back into my Facebook account. I opened the Facebook post and my jaw dropped. "Danny," I yelled out to my husband, "look at this!" I pointed to the screen just as he walked into the room. He looked at the post and then stared at me in disbelief. In a matter of hours, my post entitled "Can You Identify this Man" had hundreds of shares, likes, and comments.

Despite the initial excitement, our efforts made little progress. A year later we were still no closer to identifying the man seen that day at the dumpsite. Frustrated, I sat back on my living room couch and closed my eyes just as my oldest daughter, Lexi, walked through the front door.

"Hi Mom!" she said cheerily.

At the sound of her voice, I opened my eyes and smiled. "How was your day?"

"Long day! I'm glad to be home," she said as she plopped down on the couch next to me. She rested her head on my shoulder and pointed to the papers strewn across the coffee table. "It looks like you have been working on the Witt case," she commented.

I nodded my head.

Lexi leaned over and picked up the newspaper article and the composite sketch. "Who is this guy?" she asked.

"I wish we knew," I said. "We've been trying to find him."

"I'm sorry, Mom," Lexi's sweet voice reassured me. "Don't give up. You'll find him." She paused, laughed, and then said, "I must admit that is a really horrible sketch, though! No wonder you can't find him."

We both laughed.

"Sadly, that's all we have," I said. "And at this point, I am completely out of ideas." Our eyes met, and then it hit me like a lightning bolt! Lexi, an incredibly creative and talented artist, has been recognized throughout our community for her work. Lexi can draw, sculpt, paint, and sew. There is literally nothing she can't create.

"We could update the sketch," I said excitedly. "What I mean is—you could update it. Would you be willing to do that?" I asked.

"Me?" she asked.

"Yes, you. I trust you to do it, and I know you will do a fantastic job. It won't be a police sanctioned composite sketch, of course, but you could freshen it up—breathe some life into it for us," I said. "It might help the case."

"I would be honored to do it, Mom. I really hope it makes a difference," Lexi said.

"I really think it will," I said hopefully.

Days later, a beaming Lexi presented me with her updated version of the composite sketch. "Wow!" I exclaimed. "This is absolutely fantastic! I can't wait to see what happens when we release this. Someone is bound to recognize this man."

Later that evening, I released the original sketch side by side with Lexi's updated version on Facebook along with this explanation:

> The photo on the left is a police sanctioned composite sketch of a man that was last seen near the location where Melissa Witt's body was recovered in Franklin County in January of 1995. The photo on the right is an attempt to freshen up that composite sketch that was produced based on witness testimony. The second sketch is not police sanctioned and should not be treated as such. This is simply an attempt by our documentary team to breathe some fresh

life into a 23-year-old composite sketch. If you happen to recognize this man, please call our anonymous tip line at 1-800-440-1922.

Six days later, our first tip came through on the hotline. "He's from Conway, Arkansas," the caller said before the line disconnected. A few days later, another new lead was called into the hotline. "Looks like Larry Swearingen to me," the caller suggested, "but I don't know for sure."

"It's one of the young men she dated."

"I think it's Travis Crouch," said another caller.

"It looks like a drifter from Texas who traveled as a crew boss."

"Oh my god, it's my ex-husband!" yet another caller insisted. "It has to be him!"

And so it went. Hundreds of tips poured in from across the United States regarding the identity of the man in the composite sketch. None of the calls, however, provided definitive information.

Twenty-seven years later, the mystery remains. Who was the young man changing clothes In the Ozark National Forest that cold December day? Was he involved in the murder of Melissa Witt? Unfortunately, we may never know.

Chapter Eleven
LITTLE GIRL GONE

One hundred and forty-seven days after Melissa Witt's body was discovered in the Ozark National Forest, the unthinkable happened. Another girl vanished. Only this time the victim was a six-year-old child from a small town just under twenty miles from the site of Melissa's abduction.

On the evening of Friday, June 9, 1995, families in Alma, Arkansas enjoyed attending a favorite American pastime of little league baseball. Colleen Nick and her daughter, Morgan Chauntel, were among the nearly 300 in attendance to see the Marlins and the Pythons play one of the last games of the tournament. The duo, invited by close friends to the game, had driven from their home in Ozark, Arkansas. According to news and police reports, at around 10:30pm, Morgan and her friends asked permission to leave the safety of their parents in the stands to go catch lightning bugs. According to Colleen, she was at first reluctant to allow her small daughter to leave her side. Eventually, however, she relented, and Morgan, in her green Girl Scouts t-shirt, blue denim shorts, and white tennis shoes, happily skipped off to play with her friends. Colleen Nick didn't know that this would be the last time she would ever see the blonde-haired, blue-eyed little girl who loved cats and apples and dreamed of becoming a circus performer and a doctor.

The game ended roughly 15 minutes later. When the other children returned to the stands without Morgan, Colleen was concerned. "Where is Morgan?" she asked. According to the kids, Morgan was dumping sand out of her shoes by her mother's Nissan Stanza. Colleen raced to the car to look for her daughter. Reports indicate that Colleen "went over to the car, looked around the outside of the car, opened the doors, and looked inside the car, thinking she had gotten in. At one point, Colleen even looked under the car believing that her daughter had to be there somewhere. Within minutes, most of the parking lot was drained of people and of vehicles. It was clear that Morgan Nick wasn't there."

As Colleen frantically searched for her six-year-old daughter, a coach questioned one of the children who reported seeing a "creepy" man talking to Morgan. He immediately contacted the police. Six minutes later, authorities arrived on the scene and launched a full-scale search for Morgan. The search stretched on for days, weeks, months, and then years. And now, even two decades later, the question still remains: Where is Morgan Nick?

Former Alma Chief of Police, Russell White, was quoted as saying this about the Nick abduction:

> We have some facts about what happened that day; we don't know who took her. We've had speculation about whether it was a local person or someone just traveling through. The thing about this case is, if it was a local person, they've probably moved on or died, or been incarcerated for something else—something that has kept them from doing it again. People who do this kind of offense don't tend to stop on their own. They probably would have done it again, but they have not offended here again. But there are just too many variables to pinpoint whether it was a local person or not.

Six years after Morgan's disappearance astonishing new information was released. On January 5, 2001, The *Times Record* ran a story written by John Lyon entitled "Sketch Offers New Suspect." A quote from the article caught my eye: "The sketch is markedly different from a sketch that investigators released previously. In fact, the person in the first sketch is no longer considered a suspect."

The article went on to quote Russell White as saying, "We don't think that the first sketch is valid. This is a totally different sketch and from different people than where the first one came from. No clothing description was released with this new sketch because accounts of the man's clothing were conflicting." I was stunned. How could anyone think it was a good idea to circulate an incorrect composite sketch? How could anyone expect to find Morgan Nick that way?

According to the *Times Record* report, when asked where the information for the original composite sketch came from, White said:

> It was given [to us] by a lady that witnessed an event at a laundromat the night before Morgan's disappearance. The person in that sketch was not seen at the ballpark where Morgan Nick disappeared... the information from that sketch was not taken from witnesses at the ballpark.... Honestly, we didn't have a unanimous decision on that. There were some mixed feelings about whether to do that. In hindsight, it probably wasn't a good idea. At the time it seemed like the right way to go.

White's words, "it seemed like the right way to go," as an explanation for the composite sketch fiasco sadly reminded me of the findings from a study conducted two years after Morgan Nick disappeared. In 1997, the Washington State Attorney General's office released a report on the groundbreaking research they had conducted on 600 child abduction cases nationwide. The study found that police were generally ill-equipped to respond to these types of crimes and often failed to investigate obvious areas of importance, such as canvassing the neighborhood where the abduction took place. Overall, the study revealed that haphazard responses to child abductions were incredibly common and contributed to the inability to solve hundreds of cases across our nation.

I often wonder if the Nick case falls into this category. Did the poor decisions made early on in the investigation hurt law enforcement's chances of ever locating Morgan Nick? In my opinion, those decisions not only damaged the case, they also eroded the public's faith in their efforts. For example, shortly after Morgan's disappearance, investigators in Alma began to theorize that the Witt and Nick abductions could be related. I was skeptical as I read through the news articles and reports on the possible connection between the cases. After all, these were the same investigators responsible for circulating the wrong composite sketch in the disappearance of a six-year-old little girl!

Curious about the amount of time and resources wasted following false leads generated by the wrong sketch, I reached out to the Alma Police Department. To date, my repeated inquiries have remained unanswered.

Given that things seemed to be handled so poorly in the Nick case, I started to wonder if they could possibly be right about a connection between Morgan and Melissa. According to Jay C. Rider, he left no stone unturned and personally investigated the theory that there could be a possible connection between Morgan Nick's disappearance and the murder of Melissa Witt. "We couldn't know for sure if we had a mixed offender on our hands or not," he said. "It's rare to have an offender that targets both adults and children, but it does happen sometimes and it was suspicious that the two abductions were so close together. They were only six months apart. It had to be investigated. But after investigating every angle, I just don't feel the evidence is there to point to the two cases being linked." After spending over six years investigating the Melissa Witt abduction and murder, I wholeheartedly agree with Rider's conclusion. There is absolutely no evidence at this time that points to a connection in the two cases.

As I think back on the study conducted by the Washington State Attorney General's office, I often wonder what other critical mistakes were made in the Morgan Nick investigation. I'm particularly curious about an event that took place the same day of Morgan's abduction on June 9th.

According to reports and interviews, on that hot June summer day, something of note happened. In the parking lot of a grocery store in Alma, Arkansas, a man and a woman approached two little girls. One of the children felt anxious about the encounter so she ran inside the grocery store to find her father. Concerned for the safety of the girls, the father immediately approached the couple to find out what was going on. The man told the girls' father that he was on the run from law enforcement. His female companion was already in the truck and she refused to get out of the vehicle or make eye contact as the two men spoke.

The father, a mechanic, quickly determined that there was something very unusual and menacing about this man and this situation. He noticed that the couple's truck was towing a U-Haul trailer; however, for some reason, they had taken everything out of the U-Haul and placed it in the back of the pick-up truck. And while there is not a clear description of the woman, reports describe the man as having a very distinct mole on his face.

What are the odds of this strange interaction at the grocery store parking lot and the Morgan Nick abduction happening on the exact same day in the exact same town of less than 4,000 people? Even more alarming is the significance of the June 9th date to the Arkansas River Valley. Believe it or not, Morgan Nick was not the only child abducted on June 9th. Twelve years earlier, on June 9, 1983, Matthew Crocker, just four months old at the time, also vanished without a trace.

Unlike Morgan's case, Matthew's abduction has garnered little attention. According to law enforcement, earlier that month, Matthew Crocker's mother met a woman who called herself "Kathy Johnson." Kathy claimed to be working at a carnival in Fort Smith, Arkansas at the time. Matthew's mother needed help with child care, so she invited Kathy to stay with her family in their Van Buren home for the week.

On the evening of June 9, the Crockers hosted a party in their home. After a night of partying, Matthew's mother awoke to discover that both Kathy Johnson and her infant son were missing. Kathy had stolen a car that was parked at the Crocker home and apparently snuck away with the tiny baby in the middle of the night.

Neither Kathy nor Matthew have ever been located. Law enforcement theorize that the woman kidnapped baby Matthew to raise as her own child.

In 2019, Sergeant Daniel Perry with the Van Buren Police Department invited me to review the Crocker case files. "Kathy Johnson was believed to be around 26-years-old at the time," said Perry. "Supposedly, she had lost two children shortly before they were born. We also think she might be using the first name of Judy."

The police report describes Kathy Johnson as a Caucasian woman with dark blonde hair and a chipped or decayed front tooth. Kathy has a six to seven inch scar on her left shoulder blade and a puncture scar that is located approximately six to eight inches above her right knee. "We think this woman should be easy to identify," said Perry. "She had a tattoo of a green and yellow star or sunburst on the left side of her chest, a tattoo of a unicorn on her upper left arm and a tattoo on her upper right arm of the name 'Kathy' with a ribbon above it." Perry believes that Matthew could still be alive but does not know his original identity.

"It's also important to add," Perry said, "that Matthew suffered from a condition called pectus excavatum or concave chest. If he's out there, we should be able to identify him very easily."

I wonder how well the Nick abduction case was investigated in relation to the Crocker abduction. To my knowledge, none of the information about the situation in the grocery store parking lot in 1995 or the Crocker abduction in 1983 were ever released to the media by Alma authorities in the Morgan Nick investigation.

In all fairness, it's important to note that cases like Morgan's are incredibly rare and difficult to tackle—especially for a small town police department. Statistics show that only a fraction of 1% of children are kidnapped in stereotypical stranger abductions like that of Morgan Nick.

Each day, an average of 2,100 children are reported missing in the United States. Of this number, 800 of these cases turn out to be false alarms based on miscommunications or misunderstandings. Only a very small portion of these children are abducted by someone who is not a family member. Sadly, those children are often sexually or physically abused before being released or escaping if they are not killed.

Non-family abductions are defined as episodes in which a person who is not a family member takes a child by using physical force or threatening physical force and detains the child for a substantial period of time or where a child younger than 15 or who is mentally challenged is taken or detained by a non-family member who conceals the child, demands ransom, or expresses an intent to keep the child permanently. Non-family abductions are distinctly different from "stereotypical kidnappings."

Stereotypical kidnappings like Morgan's are almost always committed by non-family members and are considered to be more dangerous than family abductions because these cases almost always end in the child's murder. It's heartbreaking, but the reality is that Morgan Nick was most likely murdered shortly after her abduction.

Regardless, like most people in my community, I am haunted by the notion that a six-year-old girl was snatched by a stranger from a crowded ballpark on a balmy summer night without a trace. No clues. Few witnesses. Not so much as a scream. Morgan Nick simply disappeared.

I am also outraged that during the most critical days, weeks, and months of the investigation, the public was given information that "in hindsight probably wasn't a good idea." Morgan Nick deserved better. Like Melissa Witt, Morgan deserves justice. I believe both cases will eventually be solved, but until that day comes, I will continue to passionately advocate for Melissa Witt.

Over the past seven years, I have become a powerful voice in Melissa's case and have vowed to seek justice for her murder, no matter the cost. I never imagined just how high that cost could be until the afternoon I opened my email and discovered a frightening message: "Hello, LaDonna Humphrey. It's Horrorman. I know you are looking for me. Wanna come out and play?"

Chapter Twelve
HORRORMAN

As I pulled into my office parking lot, my cell phone buzzed with the all-too-familiar alert of an incoming email. The daily onslaught of emails had begun. I sighed and braced myself for the inevitable. I turned off the engine and reached for my coffee and cell phone. I took a long, exaggerated sip and opened the message. The subject line: "New Submission—Who Killed Missy Witt?" immediately grabbed my attention. Activity in the Witt case had been at a standstill for months and the possibility of a new lead was always exciting to me. "Well, let's see what we've got," I said aloud as I opened the email.

The introductory sentence, "I'm having the creepiest realization and want to share it with you in case it helps you solve the case," reeled me in. The author went on to describe their connection to the world of death fetish pornography and their concerns about its possible association with Melissa's case. The message was compelling albeit disturbing. In the seven years of working on the Witt case I had never received information quite like this. As I sat in my Suburban considering what I had just read, my phone began to ring and vibrate, demanding my attention. I took one last sip of coffee, touched up my lipstick, grabbed my things, and walked into the building. "Death fetish pornography?" I shuddered.

The rest of the day was a blur. My every thought was on the Witt case and that disturbing email. Around 8:00pm that evening, I sat down at my desk and opened my personal Gmail account. I read through the correspondence again before forwarding it on to two recipients, Detective Brad Marion and Jay C. Rider. In less than ten minutes, my phone was ringing. "Can you talk?" Rider asked.

I laughed and said, "I guess you read my email."

Over the next hour, Rider and I discussed how to proceed with this new information. We decided I should respond to the author and try to set up a phone interview. "I will work on getting the phone interview scheduled and then get back to you with what I've learned," I promised.

After we hung up, I immediately dialed a close friend. I knew that Chris, an internet technology guru, could help me. After exchanging pleasantries, I said, "I have a strange question for you."

He laughed and replied, "How strange?"

"Well," I said slowly, "don't freak out, okay? But I need to know how to safely search out information on the Internet about death fetish pornography."

Less than an hour later, a careful Internet search introduced me to a world that I never knew existed. Necro porn, also known as death fetish pornography, is exactly what it sounds like. At least one person, usually a woman, involved in the recorded sex act "pretends" to be dead. The material isn't snuff porn in which people are murdered for the viewer's pleasure. Instead, necro porn is designed for viewers with an affinity for simulated acts of murder and necrophilia. I was horrified. But, according to my research, I am not the only one disgusted by necro porn. Even the large and completely legal pornography websites such as Pornhub, xHamster, and others ban this type of content. They too, according to a quote I found in an article on vice.com, are "repulsed."

Even more disturbing is the fact that these websites sort images and movies by "kill" type categories such as stabbing, shooting, hanging, strangulation, drowning, and crucifixion. Featured scenes in the films are organized further into subcategories such as death, rape, incest, and torture.

Research suggests there may be close to 100,000 people worldwide who actively seek out necro porn. I was shocked to learn that custom death fetish movie orders are in high demand. Consumers pay anywhere from $250 to $10,000 or more to see their specific death fetish kinks come to life on film.

It didn't take long for me to discover that those involved in the necro porn culture staunchly defend their desire to fantasize about acts of murder. In fact, the owner of one discussion forum dedicated to necro porn posted this statement defending their community:

"There is absolutely nothing illegal about our community in general. We are not serial killers in the making. What would [those] idiots know about real life? They obviously believe that fantasy is real. They might as well compare us to Disney because characters die all the time in their productions!" I was stunned by the comparison between necro porn and Disney.

These communities operate on the premise that, instead of destructive or risky, death fetish fantasies and pornography are perfectly normal. According to the Hill-Link Minority Report of the Presidential Commission, eighteen separate studies have shown that "soft" porn, which involves acts between consenting adults, definitely desensitizes viewers, and may lead to extremely violent behavior. If this can happen with "soft" porn, what does that mean for "hard" core death fetish pornography that depicts murder and necrophilia?

Determined to learn more, I sought out every bit of information I could find on the harmful effects of violent pornography. According to Fight The New Drug (FTND), a non-religious and non-legislative organization that exists to provide individuals the opportunity to make an informed decision regarding pornography by raising awareness on its harmful effects using only science, facts, and personal accounts, violent pornography like necro porn isn't harmless entertainment. "It's absolutely marketing itself into peoples' real relationships and inviting them to be curious about or try things that are non-consensual and deadly."

Even Ted Bundy, an American serial killer who kidnapped, raped, and murdered approximately 30 women, recognized the dangers of violent pornography. The night before his execution, Bundy was interviewed by the founder of Focus on the Family, Dr. James Dobson. Bundy talked candidly about the effect his pornography addiction had on his life:

> Like most other kinds of addiction, I would keep looking for more potent, more explicit, more graphic kinds of material. Like an addiction, you keep craving something which is harder, something which gives you a greater sense of excitement. Until you reach the point that pornography only goes so far…

In that same interview, Bundy also said:

> I've lived in prison a long time now. I've met a lot of men who were motivated to commit violence just like me. And without exception, every one of them was deeply involved in pornography. Without question, without exception, deeply influenced and consumed by addiction to pornography.

FBI scientists at Quantico, Virginia have also weighed in on pornography and its adverse effects. In regard to the impact of pornography and the Miami Pillow Case Rapist, for example, they reported: "He dreamed of rape.

Then he eventually slipped over the threshold of fantasy into the reality of sexual assault."

Another example of the drastic impact of violent porn can be found in the Ray Bauer case. Over the span of his 29-year marriage, Bauer often forced his wife to watch hard-core porn movies with him. After, he would bound and torture his wife. In April of 1986, Mrs. Bauer, sick and tired of the abuse, shot her husband to death after one particularly violent torture episode. After the murder, a search of the house uncovered her husband's extensive collection of violent sado-masochistic pornography and instruments of torture.

Studies by the Federal Bureau of Investigation found that eighty percent of mass murderers used pornography extensively as an integral part of their murderous sexual activity, which often included serial rape-murders. Some of these killers actually photographed their dead victims and pasted cutouts of their faces on hard—and soft— pornographic photos as preparation for their next murder. The FBI and police nationwide have also reported finding extensive pornography collections in the homes of virtually every mass-murderer that they arrest. It's clear that necro porn, despite the claims to the contrary by those who consume it, is anything but an innocent fantasy.

Armed with knowledge from my research, information gleaned from the phone interview, the blessing of investigators, and sheer determination to find possible answers in the Witt case, I found the courage to set up usernames on multiple death fetish discussion forums. The information I uncovered about the necro porn culture was both shocking and frightening. Due to the sensitive nature of Melissa Witt's murder investigation, I will not share everything I learned.

(Disclaimer: Death fetish pornography is both graphic and traumatizing. I do not encourage or endorse participating in an investigation of it, or even a simple Internet search on this topic, without the consent of law enforcement and access to a therapist.)

Within minutes of joining each forum, I was immediately greeted by a host of death fetish porn fanatics hungry to devour the details of the "newbie's" fetish. My forum inbox was bombarded with explicit requests to swap stories and photos. I could feel the bile rising in the back of my throat after reading the first dozen or so private messages. "Mental note," I said to myself, "never open the forum messages again!" And I didn't.

It was impossible for me to read through every user comment within the forums. Believe it or not, each forum contained hundreds of thousands of posts. This forced me to limit my undercover investigation to three of the most "popular" sites. As I narrowed down my scope, I immediately noticed that a handful of screen names were participants in all three forums. These users spent up to ten hours each and every day discussing death fetish topics. In fact, one extremely dedicated user had a combined total of 172,315 posts across the three forums.

Within the forums, the bulk of the information is written in story form and shared by members with disturbing usernames such as LadyKiller, DeathBringer,

ChokeHerDead, and GallowsMan. The content is equally startling. Caution: The following example is graphic and frightening. One wrote:

> If I had my way, I would hold her at gunpoint and force her to strip until she is completely naked. I would tell her how she is going to die since her reaction is something I would be curious about. Then, I would make her sit down on the bed, ordering her to masturbate while telling her how I am going to rape her body once she is dead. I would then pull the trigger, sending a fatal bullet to the center of her forehead.

The story continues with a disgusting description of detailed acts of necrophilia. After scrolling through the forums for several days, it became clear that, within the death fetish communities, stories like this are the norm. In fact, this type of violent content makes up 95% of the posts that users share. One by one, the gory stories of death and sex slowly began to blend together... until the day I stumbled upon posts made by a forum member using the screen name HorrorMan.

Posts made by HorrorMan were markedly different from the others. Most of his entries lacked the specific details included in a "typical" death fetish fantasy story. In fact, his posts seemed more like a confession than a story:

"I moved out of state not long after I strangled my neighbor. I could no longer control the urge."

"My next victim was a regular jogger in the park near my apartment. I decided to hide in the bushes, ambush her, strangle her, then fuck her dead body. I buried her close by. She will never be found."

"I am looking for my next victim. It is time."

I felt a sense of dread after reading his posts. I began to meticulously search every forum for his entries. I was alarmed to discover that his posts suddenly stopped in late 2020. Where was HorrorMan? Had he been writing about real crimes? Desperate for answers, I contacted the owners of the different forums and asked for information about HorrorMan. I was shocked by the responses.

"Our forum is completely safe and you have no reason to worry about HorrorMan or anyone else. Real crime discussions are forbidden in this community. Who are you and why does this matter to you?"

"HorrorMan was banned from our forum so there will no longer be new posts from him."

"HorrorMan is harmless. Mind your own business."

"His disturbing posts caused him to be permanently banned from this community. Thank you for your inquiry."

It was clear that I wasn't the only one that felt HorrorMan might be dangerous. If the death fetish community felt the need to ban him from their platforms, there was a real problem. I immediately notified the police. Authorities took my report and encouraged me to document all of the information, including the screenshots. "There is little we can do, Ms. Humphrey," one investigator told me. "A situation like this is difficult to follow up on unless you have definitive proof that a crime has been committed. Please keep us informed if you come across anything else about HorrorMan in your investigation."

Determined to find answers, I kept digging. My blood went cold as I scrolled through his posts one afternoon. On one platform, I discovered that he had provided actual locations. He had also written a post so specific, I feared it might be about the Melissa Witt case. I documented my findings and reported it to authorities.

After exhausting every avenue researching HorrorMan, I commented on one of his posts using my undercover screen name. "Your stories are so… real. Tell me more." I wrote. I waited for days. No response.

Next, I sent him a private message on every death fetish forum he had participated in. A week passed. He never replied. Could he be incarcerated? Dead? What happened to him? "Dear HorrorMan, I am looking for you. Your stories would make the perfect film. Contact me. Come out, come out, wherever you are!" I posted.

The replies I received from other users about HorrorMan were disturbing. At least a dozen forum members contacted me and warned me to stay away from him. "He's disturbed," one warned. Others mentioned that he "seemed too dedicated to strangling women," and that his stories seemed to "cross the line between fantasy and reality." It was surreal to learn that even hard-core necro porn consumers had their limits. I think they secretly feared, like me, that he was writing about actual crimes he had committed.

A month after my initial search for HorrorMan began, my cell phone alerted me to an incoming message received in my personal email account. "Hello, LaDonna Humphrey," the message read. "It's Horrorman. I know you are looking for me. Wanna come out and play?" I sat in stunned silence. "That's impossible," I said as I frantically paid for my lunch and ran back to my Suburban. My real name and email address wasn't connected to any of the necro porn forums I'd joined as part of my investigation. I typed a text message to my friend Chris, the Internet guru. "Call me," I wrote. "It's an emergency."

Seconds later, my phone rang. As calmly as possible, I shared with Chris the events that had taken place. When I told him about the email, he took a long, deep breath before he said, "Holy shit, LaDonna. This is serious." For the next half hour, he gathered the necessary details to help him determine how exactly HorrorMan had discovered my true identity. "There is only one possible scenario," Chris said. "HorrorMan must be the owner of one or more of those forums and he tracked your true identity from the IP address [you] used when you registered for the forum."

I hung up the phone and immediately notified law enforcement. "There is no way to know if he is connected to the Witt case, let alone any crime," they said. "All we can do at this point is wait and see if he makes contact again. Report him immediately if he makes any kind of threat to your personal safety."

Next, I called Jay C. Rider. "I don't feel that you are in harm's way," Rider told me. "And I assure you that we will get to the bottom of this, okay? Do you feel comfortable moving forward? If you don't, nobody would blame you, LaDonna. Certainly not me. You have done more than your fair share to help solve this case."

"I knew the risks when I took this on," I assured Rider. "I can't and I won't give up now. I am determined to find justice for Melissa. I'm comfortable moving forward. I have to. We all do."

As I write this, we are still seeking answers about HorrorMan. We don't yet know if he is connected to the Witt case or to any other real crimes. Anything is possible. Research from more than 65 studies have shown that dangerous offenders are not only more likely to commit their crimes if they utilize pornography, but they are likely to employ violent acts after viewing pornography. Does HorrorMan fall into this category? We don't know yet.

What we do know is that roughly over two million pedophiles, rapists, sadists, and the like commit millions of crimes annually. This number only accounts for reported crimes. I suspect the total is actually much, much higher!

Pornography is not a victimless crime. Thousands have been tortured, raped, and murdered as a direct result of exposure to pornography. Both the American Psychiatric Association and the World Health Organization define "sexual sadism" as a mental disorder. Make no mistake, there is something inherently wrong with anyone who gets an erotic thrill from seeing nude women shot, strangled, stabbed, or killed.

The necro porn world is not a game or a funny joke. It's incredibly dangerous on a variety of levels and must be taken very seriously. It has taken a toll on me personally. In order to help me cope with the things I have seen and read during this investigation, I talk with a therapist weekly.

Make no mistake. Necro porn is dangerous.

HorrorMan is dangerous.

Do you know what else is dangerous? A determined woman on a mission to find justice for a 19-year-old murder victim. I refuse to give up. This chapter on HorrorMan is far from over. In fact, it's only just begun.

Chapter Thirteen
OBSESSION

Like others around the country, I'm obsessed with the story of the Golden State Killer. The work done by the late true-crime writer Michelle McNamara in the decades-long mystery is nothing short of incredible. Michelle first learned about the case from reading a self-published book written by retired detective Larry Crompton. After reading the book, a Google search brought Michelle to a message board dedicated to cold cases. The rest, as they say, is history.

Michelle grew up as the youngest of six siblings in Oak Park, Illinois. She was only 14 years old when a local jogger, Kathleen Lombardo, was killed near her home. Kathleen's murder was never solved and, according to Michelle, this event deeply impacted her life and spurred her lifelong true crime obsession.

Like Michelle, events from my childhood fueled my passion for all things true crime. I grew up in a small farming community in Southwest Oklahoma with a population of less than 200 people. The town offered little in the form of entertainment, so I looked forward to watching my dad bowl each week at Hilltop Lanes.

My last night there was bittersweet. When I close my eyes, I can picture myself as a ten-year-old girl, my curly blonde hair bouncing with every step. I had no idea I was living out the last carefree moments of my childhood.

Most of my memories of that last night are hazy. Others, however, are vivid. I can still hear the sound of crashing bowling pins mixed with the loud country music that blared from the speakers in the bowling alley. I can almost smell the scent of popcorn and hamburgers that emanated from the run-down kitchen and snack bar. And of course, I can still see his face—the man with the dark beard.

As always, my younger sister and I were excited to be at Hilltop Lanes. We whispered and giggled as we carefully carried drinks and snacks away from the snack bar. We had only taken a few steps when the man slammed into me, spilling most of my popcorn onto the floor. "I am so sorry," he said. "I am so clumsy! Can I buy you some more?"

"No thank you," I said as I strained my head, looking for my dad. "My dad is here and he will take care of it," I said flatly. It was impossible to hide my frustration and disappointment over the spilled popcorn.

"Oh, yes! I know your dad," the man smiled assuredly. "Great man! We were in the Army together."

"You know my dad?" I asked as I settled in my seat.

He smiled again. "Of course I do," he said. "I've known him for a very long time." The man sat down a safe distance away. From this vantage point, he was close enough to continue a conversation with us, but far enough away to avoid suspicion from other adults in the bowling alley. He was calculated. His every action was planned. He had done this before. The man with a dark beard was a predator.

"Your dad has told me all about you. In fact, he said you would be here to watch him bowl tonight!" he laughed. "That's why I stopped by. To say hello to you and your dad."

The man smiled as he watched my worried expression melt into one of relief. "I guess he forgot to tell me about it," I said. "He forgets sometimes." The man winked in response and cracked a joke. We both laughed.

The man continued to laugh as he looked around the room. "I'm surprised he hasn't stopped by to say hello yet," he said. "I bet he will soon." The man spoke with confidence. He relaxed and draped his arm over the chair next to him. His trick worked. He had gained the trust of an innocent young girl.

Four or five lanes down, my father looked up and our eyes met. He smiled and waved. "Hi, Daddy," I yelled as I waved. Unaware of the danger hiding in plain sight, my dad waved once more before turning back to his team. "See, I knew he would say hello," the man said. "I can tell he's glad I am here tonight." And I believed every word.

According to childluresprevention.com, the "affection lure" is a common technique employed by pedophiles looking to exploit unsuspecting children. Most victims of abuse are befriended and "groomed" over a period of hours, days, weeks, and sometimes months or years. It's common for a child predator to seize an opportunity to groom and lure a child by loitering in places where children frequent: parks, playgrounds, malls, arcades, bowling alleys, sporting events, and churches. That night at the bowling alley was the perfect storm of opportunity.

The man continued talking at length about my dad, their supposed time in the Army together, and their purported recent fishing trip. "You won't believe how big the fish is that we caught," the man said. "It was huge! You should come out to my car and see it."

As I considered his offer, I thought about my dad. "Dad loves to fish," I reasoned. "How big is the fish?" I asked eagerly.

"It's huge," he said. "You really do need to see it!"

I was engrossed in our conversation and didn't notice when my dad left his lane to walk to the bathroom. But the man with the dark beard took notice. He seized the opportunity. "Let's go see the fish right now. Let's go right now. Just follow me right outside. My car is parked around the back," he said. His voice was urgent, almost pleading. "We don't want the fish to die."

"Okay… as long as we come right back," I answered. "If we hurry." The man rose from his chair and started to make his way toward the door.

"I will be right back," I assured my sister.

"Where are you going?" she whined.

"Stay here. I'm going to see this fish. I will be right back," I promised. She continued to whine. "Okay, come on," I barked. "But you have to keep up!"

The man quickened his pace. "Come on, I really want you to see what I've got outside," he said. My sister and I followed closely behind.

Just as we reached the breezeway at the entrance of the bowling alley, the man opened the door to let me walk through. He reached for my hand just as the booming sound of my father's voice echoed through the bowling alley. "STOP. Stop right now!" he screamed.

My body tensed and froze.

The man bolted through the front door.

My sister wet her pants.

In a matter of seconds, my world was in chaos. The music stopped. A mob of men rushed out the door, yelling, "Get him!"

My dad suddenly appeared and scooped my sister and me up and away from the door. We watched as men grabbed for the pool sticks lining the wall near the entrance. The men yelled obscenities as they snatched their makeshift weapons before running out the door.

I screamed.

Eventually the police arrived. Once a report was made, we quickly left the bowling alley. I remember the sounds of my dad's sobs as he drove us home. Mom met us in the driveway with swollen eyes and a tear-stained face.

What was happening? I couldn't comprehend the gravity of events that had unfolded at the bowling alley.

"What did the man want?" I asked. My question caused my mother to weep. Later that night, my parents gently explained how "some bad guys like to hurt little girls."

I threw up.

Confused, I asked, "You mean you didn't know that man, Dad?"

"No," he said. "I have never met that man before."

"He tricked us," I cried. My tears were bitter, full of confusion and betrayal.

For weeks after, my sister and I slept in our parents' room. My entire family was traumatized. I had repeated nightmares. I never wanted to go back to the bowling alley.

When this took place, it was the early '80s, and very few people understood trauma, let alone the complexities of a traumatized child. As it turns out, for children, traumatic experiences can initiate strong emotions and physical reactions that can persist long after the event. Children may feel terror, helplessness, or fear, and have physiological reactions such as heart pounding, vomiting, or loss of bowel or bladder control. Often, like I did, children can feel overwhelmed by the intensity of their physical and emotional responses and shut down emotionally.

As an adult, I would learn that when a child experiences traumatic stress, it interferes with their daily life and ability to function and interact with others. Research shows that the way trauma manifests will vary from child to child and will depend on the child's age and developmental level. What I experienced that night at the bowling alley is categorized as an adverse childhood experience. These types of events can make trusting others an extremely complex issue. Survivors can feel isolated, unable to form healthy relationships, or in a perpetual reenactment of their childhood trauma. Sadly, my trauma from this experience eroded my ability to trust others. This distrust spilled over into every aspect of my life. Since then, I have struggled to learn to trust my friends and family, my coworkers; essentially, any person I come in contact with.

Yet, despite my own trauma, I determined, even at a young age, that I would advocate for others. Shortly after my ordeal, my family received news that the predator from the bowling alley had molested a little girl from a nearby town. Prosecutors believed my testimony in that case could help put him behind bars. I cried as my parents shared the details of what that monster did to that innocent little girl. It was terrifying, but I knew what I had to do.

My last memory of that incident is from inside a small Oklahoma courtroom. The prosecuting attorney asked me to identify the man who had shattered my childhood. I pointed to the coward sitting in the defendant's seat. "That's the man," I said. "That's him."

I walked out of the courtroom that day a changed person. I knew even then as a young girl that nothing would be the same. The world was different now. And even though this experience robbed me of many things, it also planted the seeds of my advocacy for crime victims.

My efforts, at times, are exhausting, but I can't give up. I have immersed myself in this quest to find justice for Melissa Witt. She deserves justice. I also believe her family, friends, and the community deserve justice. The value in keeping her case alive is immeasurable. It's critical to keep the tips coming in because someday the right piece of information will unlock this mystery.

Am I obsessed? Probably. But someone needs to play the role of tireless advocate for Melissa. Her life was worth that. Regardless of the cost, I will continue to fight every single day for her case to be solved

I know a large part of why I gravitate towards true crime, especially crimes committed against women, stems from what happened to me that dusty Oklahoma night at Hilltop Lanes. I often wonder what the grown-up version of myself would say to "Bubba," the predator from the bowling alley. I honestly think I would simply say, "I forgive you."

It's been quite the journey, but I have truly learned to forgive him. Also, I have used that experience as the catalyst for a large-scale campaign for justice on behalf of a girl I never knew.

I long for the day when Melissa's killer is brought to justice. I work for that end every single day. The emotions I feel about the Witt case are difficult to put into words, but I think the late Michelle McNamara said it best in her book, *I'll be Gone in the Dark: One Woman's Obsessive Search for the Golden State Killer.* "One day soon, you'll hear a car pull up to your curb, an engine cut out. You'll hear footsteps coming up your front walk.... This is how it ends for you."

And she's right. This is how it will end for Melissa's killer. Justice will prevail. It always does in some form or another. Just ask the man with the dark beard.

Chapter Fourteen
FALSE LEADS

In the Melissa Witt case, two words dredge up feelings of complete frustration for me: False leads. From the moment Melissa's case hit the headlines, red herrings emerged. And regardless of how crazy the lead appeared to be on the surface, detectives diligently investigated in hopes of uncovering that one clue that might help them catch Melissa's murderer. Sadly, red herrings can profoundly hinder progress for investigators. Often these false leads allow the real offender to evade capture.

In 2017, the first false lead in my personal investigation into Melissa's murder emerged, masquerading as the man I have dubbed as the "Mysterious Mr. Riley." His message, "I have information in the Witt murder that I can only share with LaDonna Humphrey," caught my attention. "I need to meet with her in person as soon as possible."

Safety is paramount when working a murder case, so my team and I rarely, if ever, agree to meet an informant in person. With that in mind, I politely declined Mr. Riley's demand to meet me. "Mr. Riley, I think it's important that you immediately contact law enforcement. They are better equipped to assist you."

His reply, "Don't you want to solve the Witt case?"

"Of course I want to see her case solved," I answered.

And so it went. Every week for the next six months, Mr. Riley and I exchanged messages about the Witt case. Eventually, his persistence paid off and I agreed to meet with him in person. However, as soon as I provided Mr. Riley with the location and time for our meeting, he promptly deactivated his Facebook account. I was baffled.

On a Wednesday afternoon, two years later, Mr. Riley suddenly resurfaced. He immediately resumed his demand to meet with me in person. According to Riley, he was terrified. "I fear for my life," he wrote. "The information I have in the Witt case could get me killed." His next claim was even more outrageous. "I've spent the last two years in hiding. I have important information! You need to take this seriously."

My response to Mr. Riley's wild assertion was simply, "Contact law enforcement immediately if you feel that your life is in danger!" I also provided the contact information for the lead detective in Melissa's case.

He replied immediately. "Don't dismiss me. I only trust you, Ms. Humphrey. I need to meet with you in person. Please meet with me. Please. I have photos and audio in the Witt case. I'm ready to turn these things over and I will only give them to you. This information will solve the Witt murder," he promised.

I sat back in my chair and crossed my arms. "Photos and audio in the Witt case? Impossible," I thought to myself.

"How is it possible you have photos and an audio recording in the Witt murder?" I asked.

"Meet with me and I will explain," he said.

Skeptical, yet curious, I relented and agreed to meet with Mr. Riley in person. "I will meet with you at 6:30pm in the parking lot of Central Mall in Fort Smith," I replied. "Don't be late."

"Here's a photo of the blue truck I will be driving," he offered in return. "This will make it easy for you to find me." He next insisted that I protect his identity at all costs. "I'm risking my life to meet with you. But I know it's the right thing to do," he said. "I need my identity kept top secret."

I invited one of my team members, Amy Smith, to make the hour-long trek with me from Northwest Arkansas to Fort Smith to meet the mysterious Mr. Riley. Amy, a long-time friend and trusted colleague, has been with the Witt documentary team from day one. Amy's strong investigative skills combined with her ability to problem solve has proven time and time again to be an incredible asset for Melissa's case.

As a precaution, we arrived in the Central Mall parking lot half an hour early. We drove around, surveyed the parking lot, and then parked in the center of the lot. With the doors locked and the engine running, we prepared for Mr. Riley's arrival.

By 6:45pm, neither Mr. Riley nor the blue truck had arrived.

"Let's contact him," Amy suggested.

I opened my Facebook messenger and fired off a pointed question: "Are we meeting?"

"On my way," he wrote seconds later. "I had to get a babysitter."

I looked up at Amy and said, "Apparently, he had to get a babysitter."

"A babysitter?" Amy asked.

I shrugged my shoulders.

I picked up the phone to contact the rest of the team. As an additional safeguard, Amy and I had stationed team members throughout the mall parking lot. "Riley is going to be late," I said. "Apparently he had to secure…" I almost couldn't say the words out loud… "a babysitter."

The stunned silence and stifled laughter on the other end of the phone was our breaking point. Amy and I burst into a fit of laughter.

The phone rang and interrupted our guffaws. A member of our team was calling. "There's a suspicious tan Range Rover parked near the mall exit. The tinted windows make it impossible to identify the driver or passenger," Dennis said. "We should keep a close eye on it."

We slowly drove to the opposite side of the parking lot to get a closer look. "Their engine is running," Amy observed. "That Range Rover is monitoring our movements."

Nodding my head in agreement I asked, "What do you want to bet that is Mr. Riley?"

"Let's see if we can get a tag number," Amy suggested. As we slowly eased our way in its direction, the Range Rover sped off.

Five minutes later, Riley sent another message. "Look, I came to the mall early and hid a package with the photos and audio behind the dumpster. I'm too afraid to meet in person."

Amy grabbed my phone and replied, "Which dumpster?"

No reply.

"Which dumpster?" she asked again.

No reply.

"Were you in the Range Rover?" she wrote.

Silence.

We quickly assembled our team in the back of the parking lot. "This is probably nothing more than a wild goose chase," I said. "But let's go ahead and check behind every dumpster... just in case."

After an hour of searching, we gave up. As expected, nothing was found.

It is difficult to understand what motivates someone to provide a false tip in a cold case, or in any case for that matter. I've received calls, emails, and letters from prisons, mental institutions, and psychics. Some claim to having seen Melissa's killer at the bowling alley that night, while others claim the killer confessed to them the details of her murder. You name it. I've heard it.

The most startling calls and emails, however, are from those rare individuals who try to take responsibility for

Melissa's murder. "I strangled Melissa slowly," one man said. "I just thought you should know."

Because false confessions and false leads are so common, law enforcement routinely holds back critical details of major crimes from the general public. This tactic helps authorities weed out counterfeits from the real killers. Fortunately, most false information is so outlandish that it can be easily dismissed. There are some situations, however, like the one with Mr. Riley, that can appear convincing at first blush.

Detectives have certainly had their own fair share of false yet convincing leads in the Witt case. "I've personally attempted to verify stories in the Witt case," Jay C. Rider said to me one afternoon. "Stories that later proved to be false. I've wasted valuable time on red herrings. It's frustrating. We don't have time to waste on that kind of bullshit."

Experts say often people falsely confess because of their inability to distinguish between delusion and reality. Most, I've learned, provide false information because they crave attention. Richard Ofshe, a UC Berkeley psychologist, has written extensively about false confessions. According to Ofshe, "Whenever you get cases that receive a lot of publicity, you can count on one thing. You see the walking wounded confessing or rambling on about crimes they know nothing about."

One of the most sensational cases of false confessions involves a man named Henry Lee Lucas. In the 1980s, Lucas confessed to killing almost 600 people. The Texas

Rangers closed dozens of unsolved cases as a result of those confessions. In fact, the more Lucas talked, the better treatment he received by law enforcement. For two years, he was provided with a private cell, his favorite meals, unlimited cigarettes, and strawberry milkshakes. Authorities drove Lucas all across the United States so he could reveal the locations of all of his murders. Henry Lee Lucas became an instant celebrity and was interviewed by countless people across the country.

It didn't take long for his stories to unravel. A suspicious prosecutor discovered that Lucas had received traffic tickets in other locations on the dates of some of his confessed murders. When presented with this evidence, Lucas recanted the false confessions. His excuse? "I enjoyed the attention," he said.

It is hard to believe, but a month after the strange encounter with Mr. Riley, he contacted me again. "I was at Central Mall that day two hours prior to our meeting," he wrote. "When you didn't find the package that I hid behind the dumpster, I came back to pick it up. I have the evidence with me now. I would like to meet with you. I promise to personally hand it to you this time."

"There is no evidence, Mr. Riley," I retorted.

"Meet with me and see, Ms. Humphrey," he taunted.

Frustrated by the amount of time we had already wasted on Mr. Riley, I denied his request to meet. The next day, I received a phone call from a blocked number. The caller claimed his name was Isaac and he had an "important message for Ms. Humphrey."

"Ms. Humphrey, Mr. Riley is a martial arts expert and you should listen very closely to what he knows about the Witt case. He knows who killed Melissa Witt. And he knows the person that witnessed the murder. He has photos, Ms. Humphrey. And audio."

After I pointed out the reasons why none of his claims were possible, Isaac promptly threatened to have Mr. Riley "karate chop" my entire documentary team.

I hung up.

My phone rang again.

Annoyed, I answered on the first ring. "Hello. This is LaDonna Humphrey."

"The answer to Melissa Witt's murder is in Fort Coffee, Oklahoma," the unidentified woman stated firmly. "Those people did horrible things to Melissa in Fort Coffee. I am sending a detailed email that includes the names of the men who killed her."

The line went dead.

"Fort Coffee, Oklahoma," I said to myself. "Here we go again."

The rumors that have circulated about Fort Coffee and its supposed connection to Melissa Witt have been devastating for her case. This red herring is deeply interwoven into the very fiber of Melissa's murder investigation. I knew I had to be cautious if I chose to investigate this new information about Fort Coffee. The town and the people who live there are dangerous and unpredictable.

I opened the email, determined to begin my investigation into a town infamous for prostitution, methamphetamine distribution, murder, and mayhem.

There was no going back now.

Chapter Fifteen
FORT COFFEE

Just days after Melissa disappeared from the Bowling World parking lot, law enforcement, in partnership with the local media, made a plea to the public for information. Anyone who had been to Bowling World on the evening of Thursday, December 1, 1994 was asked to call the Fort Smith Police Department.

After the broadcast, the phone rang off the hook. One caller, and then another, claimed that around 6:30pm on Thursday, December 1, they'd witnessed a white female matching the description of Melissa Ann Witt arguing with an African American male.

A composite sketch was drawn and released to the media. Incredibly, almost overnight, the story took on a life of its own. It began with whispers of drug dealers, Fort Coffee, and unpaid drug debts. Eventually those rumors morphed into tales of Melissa leading a secret life revolving around methamphetamines, sex, and shady characters.

These wild and unfounded accusations fueled the already tenuous lines of racial, religious, and socioeconomic division in Fort Smith and its surrounding communities.

"These stories coming out of Fort Coffee," Jay C. Rider said one afternoon, "were damaging to the case and hurtful to Melissa's mother. Fort Coffee is an almost entirely black community in Oklahoma. And back in 1994 if you wanted to buy methamphetamines, that's where you went. A very large percentage of the population of that community was dealing dope. I guess to make themselves look like bad asses they started these stories about how they had kidnapped Melissa Witt. This happened early on in our investigation but the rumors stuck with her case. It's a damn shame. Melissa had no connections to Fort Coffee. None!"

Rider slammed his fist down on the table for emphasis. "Melissa Witt was not involved with anyone at Fort Coffee!"

Fort Coffee, located in Le Flore County, Oklahoma, was originally constructed in 1834 as a U.S. Army fort. The town, named for U.S. General John Coffee, is tiny, covering only a total area of 6.4 square miles with a population of just over 400 people.

The small border town is anything but quaint. According to court records and news reports, it is the town to arrest methamphetamine distributors and manufacturers. In fact, one operation, nicknamed "Hell on the Border" ended with the arrest of 34 people by state, federal, and local drug investigators.

It seemed unlikely a young woman like Melissa Witt would have any ties to this dangerous community. But, as the rumors swelled, law enforcement did the only thing they could. They combed Fort Coffee, searching homes and interviewing witnesses.

During one of my interviews with former Detective Sergeant Chris Boyd, we discussed the impact the Fort Coffee rumors had on Melissa's case. "The rumors focused on the fact that Melissa was supposedly involved with drug dealers in eastern Oklahoma and she was kidnapped because of that," Detective Boyd said. "As you know, LaDonna, nothing in Melissa's background indicated that. Nothing in her circle of friends and family connected her to drugs or to Fort Coffee. We [law enforcement] spent quite a bit of time on this subject to find out where the story led. It went nowhere. There was no truth to these accusations."

Boyd was right. Every facet of Melissa's life was thoroughly investigated. There was absolutely nothing that connected her to the dangerous and illegal underworld of drugs. Later, when the medical examiner's findings were released, the toxicology report supported the work of investigators: "No drugs were found in her system."

"Absolutely nothing," said Boyd, "was found in her system. If Melissa had been involved in a lifestyle that included methamphetamines or other illegal drugs, the toxicology report would have indicated that, but it didn't. There were no drugs found in Melissa Witt's system."

Despite evidence to the contrary, the Fort Coffee rumors have managed to become a legend throughout the

River Valley. Each generation has passed down its own version of what "really" happened to Melissa Witt. The tips I've received about Fort Coffee have included stories of how Melissa was shot, stabbed, or beaten to death. Sadly, as the years go by, the stories stray further and further away from any semblance of truth.

This latest information given to me about Fort Coffee was different. The woman on the other end of the phone seemed sincere. Her voice was heavy with fear and her words tainted with urgency. "The answer to Melissa Witt's murder is in Fort Coffee, Oklahoma," the unidentified woman stated firmly. "Those people did horrible things to Melissa in Fort Coffee. I am sending a detailed email that includes the names of the men who killed her."

The caller kept her promise and immediately sent me an email. She wrote extensively about her direct knowledge of crimes committed in and around Fort Coffee, including drug trafficking, kidnapping, human trafficking, rape, and murder. She provided the names of alleged drug dealers, prostitutes, pimps, and traffickers along with names of potential victims. The frightened woman claimed to have first-hand knowledge of "what happens to white women in Fort Coffee," and shared her own personal experience in heartbreaking detail:

"Two years after Melissa was murdered, I was held captive in Fort Coffee, repeatedly drugged, raped and beaten," she wrote. "I was forced to have sex with dozens and dozens of men in a matter of a few weeks. I wanted to die. Once my captors were done with me, they wanted me to die, too." The woman, whose name I will not reveal, described how, on her last day in Fort Coffee, she was gang raped and then injected with a "hot shot." Hot shots are a technique in which a person intentionally injects their victim with enough drugs to kill them.

Next, she described how the men, believing she was either dead or would soon die, dumped her body in a ditch. "Those bastards left me in that ditch like I was a piece of garbage," she wrote. "They threw all of my belongings, including my phone, on top of my body and sped away. Thank the good Lord my phone wasn't damaged. It still had service. When I woke up, I called my brother for help. I laid in that ditch for hours until he found me. I just laid there as still as possible. I was terrified they would come back and find me.

"I've kept up with your work on the Witt case and for some reason I feel I can trust you," she continued. "I am attaching proof of everything I have described in this email." Attached to her email was a copy of the police report, hospital records, and a sworn statement from her brother. She closed her email with, "I am telling you my story, because some of these men bragged about Melissa Witt's murder. I don't know if they did it to scare me or if they were serious. But I know all too well that these men are capable of terrible things.

"There's one more thing," she added. "There's another girl you should talk to. I know her. She was trafficked and held captive in Fort Coffee in 1994. She escaped. She lives out of state and won't share her location. She has a private

Facebook account set up so she can communicate with people safely, and I don't know if she will respond to you."

Two decades ago, human trafficking was often mistaken for street-level prostitution. The rise of the Internet has all but emptied the once busy streets. Customers can go online through social media and the dark web to find girls who are being advertised online. Traffickers arrange for customers to meet up, usually inside a local hotel room. Victims are then sold between 10 to 20 times a night, for about $7500 a week.

Research shows that a typical victim is usually a teen who ran away from home, or a woman trying to escape drug addiction or an abusive partner. The traffickers are typically gang members, drug dealers, or pimps. Across the board, they promise these young women a better life that includes food, housing, transportation, and protection. Victims often don't discover they have been trapped into the cycle of trafficking until it's much too late.

While researching human trafficking statistics in Oklahoma, I came across information from the Solutions Initiatives Strategies Summit. In 2014, they presented information focused on the growing epidemic of human trafficking across the United States. The state of Oklahoma, as it turns out, is believed to play a major role in trafficking. Oklahoma cities are on major human trafficking routes throughout all ports, north, east, and west, with its three major interstate highways, I-35, I-40, and I-44, providing a crossroads. And human trafficking is big, big business. An estimated global annual profit of all human trafficking is estimated at over $31.6 billion.

The summit drew attention to the three major factors that create vulnerable populations for traffickers in the state of Oklahoma. As of 2014:

Factor #1: Oklahoma had the highest incarceration rate of women in the world. According to statistics, children without mothers in the household are six times more likely to fall into drugs, prostitution, and other crimes than other children.

Factor #2: Throughout the United States, Oklahoma was second in teen pregnancy and homeless children, therefore creating what is considered a "stable" of children vulnerable to human trafficking.

Factor #3: According to FBI reports, it was well known among truck drivers that "if you want good barbeque, go to Kansas City; if you want young girls, go to Oklahoma City."

Despite the disturbing statistics, I knew I owed it to both Melissa Witt and Jane Doe to follow up on this lead. I opened the email again, clicked on the link, and wrote an impassioned plea asking Jane Doe to contact me. Six weeks after I hit send, she responded. Over the next few days, she shared details about her time in Fort Coffee. "I am slowly rebuilding my life," she said. "I work full time and I spend every second I can with my children. I'm in therapy. It helps me deal with what I went through. I will never go back to Arkansas or Oklahoma," she added. "I just can't take that risk. I am never going back."

Jane Doe, as it turns out, was held captive in Fort Coffee, Oklahoma during the months of November and December 1994. When asked if she ever saw Melissa Witt, her response was an emphatic, "No, she was never there."

"How can you be sure?" I asked.

"I knew every girl that was trafficked during that time period," she explained. "Most of us, if not all of us, had a long history of drugs, prostitution, and petty arrests. There were a few other girls that were with me that winter. Melissa Witt was not one of them." The relief I felt in learning that Melissa was not subjected to those monsters in Fort Coffee was short-lived. After all, there were countless other women, like Jane Doe, who suffered terribly, barely escaping with their lives.

Human trafficking is a crime that is often hidden in plain sight. If I have learned anything through the course of my investigation, it's this: It is important to be aware of human trafficking warning signs. These signs that a person may be a victim of human trafficking are adapted from information provided by the Polaris Project and its National Human Trafficking Resource Center as well as Innocents at Risk:

- Appearing malnourished

- Showing signs of physical injuries and abuse

- Avoiding eye contact, social interaction, and authority figures/law enforcement

- Seeming to adhere to scripted or rehearsed responses in social interaction

- Lacking official identification documents

- Appearing destitute/lacking personal possessions

- Working excessively long hours

- Living at place of employment

- Checking into hotels/motels with older males, and referring to those males as boyfriends or "daddies," which is often street slang for pimp

- Poor physical or dental health

- Tattoos/branding on the neck and/or lower back

- Untreated sexually transmitted diseases

- Small children serving in a family restaurant

- Security measures that appear to keep people inside an establishment such as barbed wire inside of a fence or bars covering the insides of windows

- Not allowing people to go into public alone, or speak for themselves

It has been five years since Jane Doe and I first connected. Since then, she has kept in regular contact with me. It comforts me to know she is safe and it is inspiring to watch Jane Doe overcome the terror and torment she endured inside that run-down trailer in Fort Coffee so many years ago. She's the true definition of a survivor.

I've experienced so much since diving headfirst into the world of advocacy. I've experienced joys and successes, along with disappointment and heartbreak. I've learned that the pursuit of justice is multi-faceted and that stories of injustice, like that of Melissa Witt and Jane Doe, often intersect. And while it is not possible for me to carry the anguish of every inequity I encounter, what I can do is use it as my fuel to continue this quest on behalf of Melissa Witt.

Chapter Sixteen
JUSTICE

James Renner, author of *True Crime Addict* and founder of The Porchlight Project, a nonprofit dedicated to offering support for the families of the missing and murdered, once told me that "when it comes to solving crime, every case is a race against the clock from the second the call comes in. As the years tick by and leads turn cold, it takes fearless dedication to dust off the case files and fight for justice." Now, in my seventh year of working on the Melissa Witt case, I can better appreciate the wisdom James shared with me that afternoon. This work is not for the faint of heart.

Unsolved cases like Melissa's strike a chord with me. They represent cruel tragedy and heartbreak. These crime victims deserve justice. Unfortunately, that's not always a possibility. The National Institute of Justice estimates that fewer than 20 percent of agencies have adequate systems and protocols in place to investigate long-term cold cases. Very few departments have dedicated cold case detectives, and almost every agency lacks resources to pay for overtime or lab fees to process evidence when new technology comes along. To bridge this gap, true crime advocates across the United States have stepped up, diligently working to crack cold cases. Among the most notable are podcasters. Through podcasts, true crime fans and advocates learn about unsolved cases, but often take it a step further to become actively involved in propelling cold cases toward justice. Podcasts connect listeners and create large networks of criminal justice reform advocates.

In 2017, I discovered this power when I was invited to discuss the Melissa Witt case on the *True Crime Garage* podcast. *True Crime Garage* is not only one of the most downloaded podcasts of the true crime genre, it is also one of the most respected. The hosts of the show, Nic Edwards and The Captain, captivate audiences with passionate storytelling techniques that showcase their journalistic and investigative skills.

I reached out to Nic with *True Crime Garage* after his podcast covered the story of Gary Michael Hilton, the man dubbed as the National Forest Serial Killer. Hilton is currently serving out four life sentences for homicides he committed between 2007-2008. And he remains a suspect in several other unsolved murders. As part of his research for that episode, Nic looked for cases of unsolved homicides that involved National Forests, specifically in the southern region of the United States.

As an aside in the story about Gary Hilton, Nic mentioned Melissa Witt's unsolved murder. According to

Nic, "Because Melissa was found near the Ozark National Forest, I thought maybe she could have been one of Hilton's earliest victims." After listening to the podcast, I contacted Nic via email. I introduced myself and immediately dove into a detailed explanation of why I believe Gary Hilton isn't a viable suspect in Melissa's murder. To my surprise, Nic responded quickly and agreed to schedule a phone call with me. "Can you talk on Thursday?" he wrote. "I would like to discuss this in detail while also learning more about Melissa Witt's case."

I cleared my calendar, and on Thursday when the phone rang, I picked up on the second ring. "This is LaDonna Humphrey."

"Hi, LaDonna. It's Nic Edwards. Thanks for taking my call."

Over the next hour, Nic and I discussed Melissa's case, *True Crime Garage*, and our shared passion for true crime. The conversation was fascinating. Nic and I discovered that we both take a similar intellectual approach to investigating cold cases based on victimology and the perpetrator's method of operation. As the discussion came to a close, Nic said, "Listen, I think you would be a great guest for the *True Crime Garage* podcast. Is that something you would consider?"

At the time, I knew very little about the *True Crime Garage* podcast, but I immediately accepted Nic's offer. "Thank you so much! I absolutely will," I said. "I think the opportunity could be fantastic for Melissa's case." I had no idea just how prophetic those words would prove to be.

About a week later, we spent roughly two hours recording the two-part podcast. Throughout that process, Nic and I became fast friends. We agreed to stay in touch and I promised to call him with any major developments in Melissa's case.

Several weeks later, in November of 2017, the first segment of the podcast aired. When it launched, I was on location in the Ozark National Forest working with my documentary film crew on "Uneven Ground: The Melissa Witt Story." Because phone service in that area of the national forest is basically nonexistent, I had left my cell phone in the truck. After six hours of filming, we called it a day and packed up our gear to make the trip back to Northwest Arkansas. Once we reached the Interstate, I powered my cell back on. Within minutes, hundreds upon hundreds of notifications lit up my phone.

I distinctly remember Amy asking me, "What on earth is happening with your phone?"

"I don't know," I responded. "I have over 1100 Facebook notifications, 56 missed calls, 35 Witt hotline calls, over 400 unread emails, and 72 text messages. I don't even know where to begin."

Amy and I looked at each other in disbelief. It didn't take long for me to discover that the overwhelming amount of activity was a direct result of the podcast. Melissa's case was suddenly receiving attention from true crime enthusiasts all across the United States. This was a breath of fresh air for a case that essentially no longer had national media coverage. In fact, as the years had stretched on, even local media outlets reported less and less on Melissa's unsolved murder. But the winds of change arrived when the *True Crime Garage* podcast aired. Melissa Witt's case would, thankfully, never be the same again.

To draw even more attention to Melissa's case, I began to share the story of both her life and her untimely death on the "Who Killed Missy Witt" Facebook page I created in October of 2015. I began by sharing photos, conducting interviews, and engaging readers by asking for their participation in sharing posts and answering questions. I also frequently shared my relentless passion in finding justice in this decades old case. The Facebook page steadily grew from 100 to well over 12,000 dedicated followers, and many of our posts have been shared millions of times. As the army of advocates demanding justice for Melissa Witt expanded, tips came flooding in. "If it weren't for these efforts," Jay C. Rider told one reporter, "law enforcement would not have a fraction of the information we now have in the Witt case. We have received solid leads that could very well lead to the resolution of Melissa's case once and for all. I am grateful to LaDonna Humphrey for keeping this case alive."

My efforts, however, do not go unchecked. To be effective, it's been important that I work closely with both the current and retired detectives on Melissa's case. Building trust has been paramount, and I abide by an important set of rules: All information I receive about the Witt case is immediately shared with detectives, and I never, ever reveal details about the case without express consent. Jay C. Rider has also spent an extensive amount of time teaching me how to pursue tips, check facts, and stay accountable. This unlikely marriage of a true crime advocate with seasoned detectives has grown solid over time. We communicate regularly, make important decisions together, and often participate in media interviews as a team. We are unified in our goal: Justice for Melissa Witt.

The responsibility I have in this murder case is often an incredibly heavy burden. The work is hard, sometimes thankless, and usually all-consuming. My very public work on this case has created a scenario where my every action and motive is closely scrutinized by thousands of people almost daily. Every single word I post on Facebook or speak on a podcast or in a media interview comes with a consequence. I am impacting the public's perception of both Melissa Witt's life and her unsolved murder. It's important that the public sees Melissa Witt as the 19-year-old girl who was brutally victimized, and not as a story to quench their insatiable thirst for true crime entertainment. This is a real story about a real person whose life was stolen. It's necessary to share details of Melissa's murder in my quest for justice, but it's also equally important for me to choose my words carefully and tastefully in order to protect her memory. For example, I never share crime scene photos and I rarely, if ever, go into the gruesome details surrounding the discovery of Melissa's body in the Ozark National Forest. Those details are not necessary in propelling her case to justice.

It is no secret that true crime is big business. The business of discussing the details of horrific stories of murder and mayhem has grown at a rapid rate over the last decade. Every platform imaginable is brimming with stories of true crime including podcasts, Twitter, Facebook, Netflix, YouTube, television, and on and on and on. The public's demand for true crime is at an all-time high. The documentary *Making a Murderer* is an example of that demand. Over 18 million viewers watched that documentary in the first month of its release. Eighteen million! Can you imagine what that kind of audience could do for an unsolved murder case like Melissa's?

The hope of what could be fuels my drive to bring awareness to Melissa's case. My advocacy, while sometimes misunderstood and criticized, does bring considerable benefits. It has educated the public on the complexities of Melissa's case while also addressing the severity of the damage that can stem from misinformation and false leads. Most importantly, these efforts have been the catalyst for conversations that might not have happened elsewhere. In turn, these have opened the doors for opportunities to discuss Melissa's case on multiple podcasts, in television interviews, radio interviews, and in magazine and newspaper interviews.

As I contemplated how to leverage the new laser-focused attention on Melissa's case, I was reminded of a quote from the movie A Star is Born: "Having something to say and a way to say it to have people listen to it, that's a whole other bag. And unless you get out and you try to do it, you'll never know. That's just the truth." As a writer, director, and public speaker, I have something to say and a growing platform to share that message: **Melissa Ann Witt deserves justice**.

The quest for justice in Melissa's case has also given birth to a national effort dedicated to finding justice for female strangulation cases in general in the United States. All the Lost Girls, a 501(c)(3) nonprofit organization, was founded in 2020 in memory of Melissa Witt. All the Lost Girls provides a variety of resources ranging from critical funding for DNA testing and investigative resources to national public awareness campaigns on social media. In December 2021, All the Lost Girls launched its first public awareness campaign in conjunction with the 27th anniversary of the abduction and murder of Melissa Witt by unveiling twelve billboards in Fort Smith with a simple, yet powerful message: Who Killed Melissa Witt? Someone knows.

Determined to enhance the investigative efforts for *All the Lost Girls* and in the Witt case, in June 2021, after several months of studying, I signed up to take the Arkansas state private investigator's licensing exam. I vividly recall sitting in the lobby of the Arkansas State Police Headquarters nervously awaiting my results. I'd studied for the exam with zeal, but the test proved to be much harder than I'd anticipated. I sat quietly, holding my head in my hands, hoping and praying my efforts had paid off. Roughly a half an hour later, I could hear the echoing footsteps of the proctor as she walked down the long hallway to the lobby. "This is it," I thought to myself and stood up.

"Congratulations, Investigator Humphrey," the proctor offered up as she handed me a packet of information. "You are now a licensed investigator!"

I walked out of the State Police Headquarters convinced that a perfect storm was finally brewing in Melissa's case. All of the hard work and relentless dedication to her unsolved murder was now paired with important tools that could further wage war on this injustice and ultimately reveal to the world the one thing I am determined to find: Who Killed Melissa Witt.

Chapter Seventeen
PROFILE OF A KILLER

Profiling is a technique used to identify a perpetrator of a violent crime by identifying their personality and behavioral characteristics based upon an analysis of the crime committed. The profiler, usually a specially trained FBI agent, reviews the crime scene, autopsy reports, and information about the victim to build a criminal profile.

Once the analysis is complete, an offender is categorized in one of three ways. The first is known as an organized offender. This type of killer is considered to be more sophisticated because his crimes show evidence of a great deal of planning. These types tend to be of average or better intelligence, employed, married with families and/or active in social circles. Organized offenders prepare extensively and often take the time to rehearse their well thought out plans. This type of killer is likely to have a dumpsite selected prior to committing their crimes, will generally hide or dispose of the body, and avoids leaving any evidence behind.

An organized kill will typically have three crime scenes:

1) Where the victim met the killer

2) Where the victim was killed

3) Where the victim was buried or the body was hidden

It is important to note that this type of criminal is also far more likely to revisit the scene or keep a trophy from the victim as a way to relive the murder. For all these reasons, investigators often pay close attention to the first known murder of an organized serial killer. Their first murder is usually sloppy in comparison to subsequent kills, as the killer grows more confident with each and every kill.

The second category is known as the disorganized offender. These criminals are known to be loners, usually living alone or with a relative. Typically, these offenders possess lower-than-average intelligence, struggle with mental illness, and are often unemployed or work at menial jobs. Disorganized offenders act impulsively, rarely utilizing a well-rehearsed plan to gain their victim's confidence. Instead, this type of offender acts suddenly and violently in order to overwhelm their victim and their crime is almost always messy and chaotic. A disorganized killer tends to leave the body at the crime scene, often engaging in post-mortem sexual contact with the victim.

The last type of offender leaves behind a variety of mixed messages at the crime scene. The "mixed" offender shows evidence of planning with a sophisticated MO but the assault itself is often frenzied or messy, which usually indicates the offender has only a small measure of control over their deep-seated, violent fantasies.

After reviewing Melissa Witt's abduction and murder, an FBI profiler determined that her killer was most likely a mixed offender that had the characteristics of a "beer-drinking womanizer who drove a big truck, was a macho man with many girlfriends, a police-groupie and a sportsman." Melissa's assault in the Bowling World parking lot was the truest definition of a frenzied, messy attack by a man who had very little control at the crime scene. "It's clear to me," Jay C. Rider said to me one afternoon, "the man who attacked Melissa did not plan to attack her in the bowling alley parking lot. He left too much evidence behind. He acted from a place of absolute rage." I agree with Rider's assessment. Melissa's killer was impulsive. His plan was not professional or well-rehearsed. It was a sloppy and hurried attempt to overpower a 19-year-old girl who wounded her killer's ego by showing no interest in his advances.

Determined to learn more, I asked to meet again with retired Detective Chris Boyd. As I sat in his home office one afternoon, he walked me through the basics of criminal profiling. "The basic premise in profiling," Boyd said, "is simple. Behavior reflects personality." For example, an FBI profiler gleans insight into the personality of a killer through questioning his behavior at four different phases of the crime:

1) Antecedent: What fantasy or plan (or both) did the killer have in place before he acted? What triggered the killer to finally act?

2) Method and manner: What type of victim (or victims) did the killer select? What was the method and manner of the murder? Strangulation? Stabbing? Something else?

3) Body disposal: Did the murder and the disposal of the body take place at one crime scene or in multiple places?

4) Post-offense behavior: Is the killer trying to inject himself into the investigation by reaching out to the media or to investigators?

As the retired detective and I discussed the intricacies of criminal profiling in context with Melissa's murder, he suddenly leaned in closer, looked me squarely in the eyes, and said, "Do you want to know my theory in the Witt case?"

I sat up straight, completely taken off guard. "Yes, of course," I replied. "I absolutely do."

"My theory is pretty simple. I believe that Melissa was killed by someone who not only knew her, but knew her well," he said.

Boyd had my full attention and he knew it. It's no secret that I've long suspected that Melissa knew her killer intimately. As I reached for my notebook, I asked one of the many questions that has haunted me in the case. "Do you think he planned to kill her all along?"

"I think the person who kidnapped and murdered Melissa knew where she would be and when she would be there," Boyd said. "I don't believe her killer intended for the events that transpired that night to end in her death. I think he was already there—at Bowling World—waiting for her to visit her mother like she so often did."

"And the argument in the parking lot?" I asked.

"I think the initial meeting went bad," Boyd said. "As you know, there was some shouting, or very loud talking happening, and I think this caused him to strike her to make her quit making any noise. I think he wanted to make her go with him."

Never looking up from my notes, I launched into my next burning question, "Why do you think he chose the Ozark location?"

Boyd thought about his answer carefully. "Well," he said, "I think he began driving and trying to figure out in his 'unorganized' mind what he should do next. I think her killer was familiar with the Ozark National Forest and its logging roads. I can't see a random serial killer committing the kidnapping and murder AND being capable of driving as deeply into the Ozark Mountains as this guy did. Can you?"

"No, I really don't see a random serial killer doing that," I said. "But," I said slowly, "what if a serial killer was familiar with the Ozark National Forest? Or national forests in general? What if his job brought him to the River Valley and to the Ozark National Forest?"

Boyd strummed his fingers on his desk. "It's possible," he said. "We definitely can't rule it out. But it's unlikely. A real long shot."

"Boyd's right," I thought to myself. According to the Behavioral Science Unit of the FBI's Training and Development Division, most serial killers are Caucasian males, and 85 percent are found in the United States. What's even more frightening is that at any given time it is believed that there are between 30-50 active unidentified serial killers. They appear to be normal and even charming as they go about their business of stalking their prey.

Multiple studies have found that while killing is about control, a serial killer almost always kills for one of two basic reasons: the sheer pleasure of killing or personal gain such as revenge or money. Furthermore, serial killers also generally fall into one of three types:

1) Thrill Seeker: This type of killer sees the whole process as a game. They enjoy the attention that they receive from the media, and they thrive on police pursuit and evading authorities. Thrill seeker killers will keep a record of their kills and sometimes send taunting messages to their pursuers or the media.

2) Mission Oriented: These killers think they are doing society a service by getting rid of certain members of the population.

3) Desire Power and Control: This serial killer enjoys the control he maintains over his victim. He likes

their terror and suffering, enjoys their screaming and begging for mercy.

Studies also show that serial killers will often keep mementos of their kills. Generally these fall into two categories: souvenirs and trophies. Police classify a souvenir as a personal item from the victim by which the killer can relive memories of the ordeal. Trophies are generally something the killer can use to build a shrine. These may be the victim's body parts, photos, or pieces of hair or skin.

"The killer kept Melissa's clothes, shoes, and her Mickey Mouse watch," I said. "What do you think that says about him?"

"I think her killer most likely disposed of her clothes and shoes, but kept the watch as a memento," Boyd said. "It's possible a serial killer is responsible and kept the Mickey Mouse watch as a trophy, but it's more likely it was kept as a memento."

"A memento?" I asked.

"Yes," Boyd answered. "I think Melissa's killer knew her well and kept her watch so he could always remember Melissa. I believe he cared deeply for her at one time."

Boyd seemed to anticipate my next question of "How do you think this fits in with the FBI profile?" and answered before I could formulate the words. "Many young men go out with high school and college friends deep into those mountains or along the Mulberry River to canoe, shoot, hunt, or drink beer and smoke pot. Some even take young women out there for a 'make out' session. They choose these surroundings on purpose. They know full well that law enforcement rarely has the manpower or the resources to patrol that area. That seems to be the most likely reason Melissa's body was placed where it was. The killer knew both Melissa and the Ozark National Forest very well. I think that our suspect fits the FBI profile exactly—a beer drinking, womanizing, country boy who loved the outdoors." I nodded my head in agreement. His theory matched up with the evidence and it also dovetailed with the FBI profile of Melissa's killer.

My stomach churned as I reread the words I had written as Boyd detailed his thoughts: Melissa knew her killer! I closed my notebook, thanked Boyd for his time, and stood to leave. As we walked toward the front door, the former detective shook my hand, then hugged me. "You're going to get this guy," Boyd assured me. "Just keep chipping away at this case just like you have been. It's going to happen. Don't give up."

"I won't," I promised him. "I can't let this go."

As I drove home from my meeting with Chris Boyd, his words, "Melissa knew her killer," kept playing back over and over in my mind. My thoughts began to drift back to the dozens of spiral bound notebooks stacked on my desk—each one brimming with handwritten notes about the Witt case. I recalled that the last time I flipped through their worn pages, I discovered a familiar name—a man that contacts me frequently to discuss Melissa's murder. I vividly remember the reaction of Jay C. Rider to the mention of this man's name. Could this man be connected to Melissa's murder?

As soon as I got home, I opened my top desk drawer and took out a dry erase marker. I wrote the names of four men who could be responsible for Melissa's murder on a large whiteboard. "Melissa knew her killer," I said to myself as I reached for a thick folder marked "Women and Violence." A report fell out as I picked up the bulging file:

> Over half of the killings of American women are related to intimate partner violence, with the vast majority of the victims dying at the hands of a current or former romantic partner, according to a new report released by the Centers for Disease Control and Prevention today. The CDC analyzed the murders of women in 18 states from 2003 to 2014, finding a total of 10,018 deaths. Of those, 55 percent were intimate partner violence-related, meaning they occurred at the hands of a former or current partner or the partner's family or friends. In 93 percent of those cases, the culprit was a current or former romantic partner. About a third of the time, the couple had argued right before the homicide took place, and about 12 percent of the deaths were associated with jealousy.

I could hear Boyd's voice again, "Melissa knew her killer," as I placed the folder back on my desk. Even the

CDC report seemed to confirm that Melissa knew her killer. But how?

As I sat back in my chair, I noticed a second loose paper had fallen to the floor. I picked it up. It was an email from one of Melissa's relatives:

> We never fully recovered after Melissa's death. None of us. Thank you for having the concern for justice. As the family, we just know that she is gone and justice will not bring her back or bring us 'closure,' as some suggest. Death is closure.

"Someone that knew Melissa Witt stole her life and her family," I said out loud. "She knew her killer!"

My words echoed across the empty room just as my phone rang.

The words "Unknown Caller" flashed across the screen.

"This is LaDonna Humphrey," I said. "How can I help you?"

"Hi, LaDonna. You don't know me," a woman's voice whispered. "But I've been watching all of your work on the Witt murder case. I need to tell you about a man that I dated. You won't believe this but he... he also knew Melissa Witt. That's not all. He... he also hurt me."

"He hurt you?" I asked. "What happened? Can I have his name?"

Nothing could prepare me for what she said next. "His name?" she said. "His name is..." Instinctively, I looked up at my white board just as she whispered one of the very names I had written down earlier that day.

My jaw dropped. I was completely silent.

"LaDonna? Are you there?" she asked. "I'm not the only woman he's hurt either," her voice pleaded. "There are other… victims"

I quickly rebounded from the shock of her words and said, "I'm here. I'm listening."

For the next two hours, this woman bravely described the horrible things she had endured at the hands of this monster. A monster that also knew Melissa Witt. At the end of our call I thanked her for finding the courage to come forward, and I promised to help, even if he had no connection to the Witt case.

As soon as we hung up, I immediately called Jay C. Rider. After sharing every detail of what the woman told me, he said, "Well, LaDonna Humphrey, what you've just described to me could very well be the profile of our killer. What do you think?"

"I think…" I said and then paused. "I think I need to prepare myself."

"Let's make a plan," said Rider. "But before we do, I've got a question for you. You didn't tell her that he's been calling you for several years, did you?" Rider asked.

"I didn't say a word," I assured him. "I didn't want to scare her."

"Good," Rider replied.

"What's next?" I asked

"We wait for the hot-tempered, beer-drinking, womanizing outdoorsman to call again," he responded.

"What if he doesn't call?" I asked.

"Oh, he'll call," Rider promised. "At this point, I don't think he can help himself."

Rider was right on the money. Four days later, he called.

"Hey, LaDonna," the all too familiar voice sang out. He sounded almost joyful. He was excited to talk to me. I shuddered. "How are you? I've been thinking about you and the Witt case. Any new developments?" he asked.

"Oh! Hello!" I answered. I tried to hide the disgust and fear in my voice. "I am doing well. It's so… so good to hear from you," I said, stumbling over my words. "And, about the Witt case… I am so glad you asked," I replied. "The case is really heating up."

"Oh really?" he asked. "It's heating up? What's going on? You know how much I care about this case."

"Oh, I know you do. So you will be glad to know," I replied, trying to sound casual, "we've been working on a more accurate profile of Melissa's killer."

You could have heard a pin drop. Except for the sound of his steady, shallow breathing, the line was silent for several minutes. And then suddenly, as if to mock me, he said, "The profile of the killer, huh?"

"Yes, that's right," I goaded. "The profile of the killer."

Chapter Eighteen
DETECTIVE BOYD

When I first sat down to interview the former Fort Smith Detective Chris Boyd in 2015, he projected not only strength and determination, but also a rare approachability that was in stark contrast to Jay C. Rider's tough and intimidating demeanor. Interviewing the two seasoned detectives was an honor. It was fascinating to hear first-hand accounts of their experiences as detectives in the major crimes unit. Their stories, sometimes dark, other times humorous, painted a picture of how the two men forged an unlikely lifelong friendship in the midst of serving their community and keeping dangerous criminals off the street.

"I've known Jay C. Rider since the late '70s," Boyd said. "He has always been known for his great sense of humor… and the fact that he is completely fearless. He was always ready for a fight." Boyd smiled as he recounted stories of his friend and former colleague. "We didn't actually become 'close' friends until we started working together in Major Crimes. And we very quickly discovered that we could benefit from a 'ham and egg' type of relationship. I had been a detective longer than Rider, so I kept him grounded with legalities and proper procedures.

"Rider saw our cases very differently than I did," Boyd explained. "His narcotics background and experience led him to be a whiz with informants and interrogations. His outside-the-box detective work blended well with my formal and traditional methods. We were a great team."

"How would you describe Rider on a personal level?" I asked.

"That's easy," Boyd laughed. "A man with boundless energy. Fun, entertaining, and completely loyal. That's why we're still friends," Boyd said. "He's one of the good guys."

Boyd, also one of the 'good guys,' took his oath to protect and serve his community in 1975, embarking on a career that would span several decades and impact hundreds of lives.

During his career, Boyd heroically assisted in countless emergency scenes, and worked to solve various crimes ranging from burglaries and homicides to sexual assault cases. According to Jay C. Rider, "Boyd was a compassionate yet tough detective who truly loved his job.

"He put his life on the line every day," Rider said, "and he never gave it a second thought. It was an honor to work alongside him."

Boyd retired from the Fort Smith Police Department in 2014 at the rank of Major and as a Patrol Division

Commander. He credits his wife Pam of 48 years for making it possible for him to chase his dreams. "She is a true law enforcement spouse who has maintained our children and household for almost five decades of my career," Boyd said. "While I have traveled all over the River Valley and sometimes the United States working cases, Pam has remained my steadfast partner and teammate. She never once, even to this day, complained about my job or asked me to quit."

Boyd pointed to a photo in his home office and added, "Pam and I also raised two great sons together. Both are in law enforcement." Boyd beamed with pride. "Chris Jr. is an accomplished officer, detective and SWAT Team Leader. Joey, my youngest, is also an accomplished detective, as well as an interrogator and K-9 officer."

"Any grandchildren?" I asked. Boyd smiled, nodded, and said, "I have three grandchildren. Brodie, Jocelyn and Drake. They are all great kids. I love my family. There is nothing I wouldn't do for them."

"What about you?" I asked Rider. "Tell me more about your sweetheart."

Rider's face softened as he reflected on his longtime love, Marlena Yarberro. "She puts up with me somehow," he joked. "But seriously," he added, "she stands by me and there is nothing I wouldn't do for her."

The two men shifted in their seats, uncomfortable about exposing the tenderness they usually kept hidden under their gritty exteriors. I quickly changed the subject and asked, "What about disagreements?"

"With each other?" Rider chuckled. The two men looked at each other and laughed.

"We've had our fair share of them," Boyd offered, "but we respect each other enough to not allow a disagreement to impact our personal or professional relationship."

The retired detectives were quick to point out the one topic they never disagree on—justice for Melissa Witt.

"We're not giving up," Boyd said as he looked me squarely in the eye. "I will work on this case until it's solved. That young girl deserves justice."

Boyd's words of determination aren't just for show. Both he and Rider have dedicated the last two decades of their lives to finding answers in Melissa's unsolved murder. They consult with the current lead on Melissa's case, Detective Brad Marion, to review new leads, interview persons of interest, provide guidance, and answer important questions about the investigation.

"We'll help as long as we are physically able and as long as the department will allow it," Rider said. "You know my thoughts on this, LaDonna," he added. "I won't ever give up."

Boyd nodded his head in agreement.

"For what it's worth, I think your efforts have been herculean, LaDonna," Boyd added. "You have remained dedicated to keeping her investigation alive. I fear if not for you, this case would be long forgotten."

I shifted nervously in my seat. "Thank you," I said as I shuffled through my interview notes to fight back my emotions. "I'm humbled you would say that. I just want to make a difference and see the case solved."

"I'm curious about something," I said. "If you could say something—anything—to Melissa's killer, what would you say?"

"We are not going to quit," Boyd said instinctively. "I want the killer to know that he should not feel safe. Someone knows who he is and what he did. Eventually, we'll knock at his door."

"Wow," I remarked. "That's an incredibly powerful message."

"It's just the truth," Boyd said. "Time is not on the killer's side. We are getting closer and closer every day. His time is running out."

Many years have passed since those initial interviews with Jay C. Rider and Chris Boyd. But regardless of how much time passes, both men have remained committed to their ruthless pursuit of justice. Eventually, the investigative work of these remarkable now-retired detectives will unveil the identity of a killer who has eluded capture for over two and a half decades.

A quote by the author James Renner seems to beautifully foreshadow the fate of Melissa Witt's killer: "When you're lost in the middle of a set of dominoes, you can't see the pattern that's forming in the falling blocks around you." I wonder, can Melissa's killer see that the shadowy path he navigates is paved with a landmine of carefully constructed dominoes set to collapse at his first misstep?

In a dream, I hear the heavy thuds of a row of dominoes falling over one by one, leading to her killer. I follow the path and find him lying in the very spot where he placed Melissa's lifeless body. I move in closer. His face is covered by leaves and other debris. He is motionless.

Suddenly, Rider and Boyd appear. They stand next to me. Behind them, a host of men and women are crying out for justice.

Rider growls "Let's cuff the bastard," and takes a step toward Melissa's killer.

Boyd motions for him to wait. "Let's leave him there, naked, exposed and subjected to the unforgiving elements—the same way he left Melissa."

Rider nods, steps aside, and allows the angry crowd to move in.

I awaken from my dream, flooded with a sense of relief.

"Justice," I whisper. "Justice is coming."

Chapter Nineteen
TICK TOCK

One of the most highly publicized aspects of Melissa's unsolved homicide centers around the items missing from the crime scene: Her clothing, shoes, and jewelry—specifically, a Mickey Mouse watch with a brown band. Investigators are convinced that Melissa's killer kept the watch as a way to memorialize his crime against the 19-year-old teenager. "He never wants to forget Melissa," Jay C. Rider said during an interview. "That watch gives the killer a sense of power and control while helping him to relive the crime over and over again."

"Relive the crime?" I asked. My heart sank. This was similar to what Chris Boyd had told me.

Rider, visibly struck by the harsh reality echoing through his own words, looked down at his hands as he responded. "I believe that's the most likely scenario," he said. "Her killer wants to relish in the excitement he felt that night. He enjoyed what he did, and he can remember that feeling every time he looks at her watch." Rider paused and then said, "Believe it or not, that kind of behavior is not unique. This kind of thing happens all the time."

Could someone really find pleasure in reliving the sudden violent death of a teenage girl? Unfortunately, the answer is yes. Research indicates that murderers frequently keep "souvenirs" or "mementos" after committing some of the most heinous and despicable acts known to man. In fact, items such as underwear, the victim's hair or, as in the case of Melissa Witt, jewelry, are some of the most common mementos kept by a killer.

Later, I stumbled upon the work of another expert in criminology, Dr. Tyrone Kirchengas. His research suggests that souvenirs and mementos are a sign of a killers' belief they won't get caught. According to Kirchengas, keeping a memento is part of a psychopath's overconfidence—they actually believe their manipulation or charm will prevent others from seeing the truth behind their horrific actions.

As I processed all of the information I had learned, I sent Rider this text: "It's hard to sleep at night. I can't help but wonder if that monster is running his fingers across the delicate band of Melissa's watch right at this very moment."

His reply: "My guess is that is exactly what he's doing. That watch helps him remember every single thing that happened the night he murdered Melissa."

The next morning, I carried Rider's words with me as I walked into the Fort Smith Police Department. As I made my way through the detective's division, I was overcome with exhaustion and dread. The horrific details surrounding Melissa's murder were clearly taking a toll on my emotions.

"Wow, you look like shit," Detective Williams said as I sat down inside his cramped cubicle.

"Thanks, Troy," I laughed as I shook my head at him in disgust. "Seriously, though, I've not been sleeping well."

"Murder cases will do that to you," Williams said. "But hey, at least you fit in with the rest of us now. None of us sleep well and we all look like shit."

We both laughed.

Williams leaned back in his chair and asked, "What's on the agenda for today, Humphrey?"

I glanced around the cubicle and quietly responded with, "I don't know. I guess," I paused, "I want to look at it all again. Make sure I didn't miss anything."

"You got it," Williams responded as he placed a stack of files on the desk in front of me. "Oh, and don't forget this," Williams said as he handed me Melissa's diary.

I flipped through the pages before landing on an entry from December 1993 that took my breath away. Melissa, in her own precise, feminine handwriting, was excitedly describing how she had received the Mickey Mouse watch as a Christmas gift. I winced as I read through the words Melissa penned in that innocent passage. She had no idea that 338 days after writing this entry, her cherished watch would be stolen by the same man who would also take her life.

Incensed, I closed the diary. "It disgusts me that Melissa's killer stole her watch," I said as I looked Detective

Williams squarely in the eye. "If Boyd and Jay C. are right about the killer's affinity for the Mickey Mouse watch... could it be possible that someone has seen him with the watch in the past twenty years?"

"It's possible," Williams responded. "But I am not sure how we could get someone to come forward with that kind of information."

"I do," I said. "I have an idea."

"Let's hear it," Williams offered.

"My team could offer a reward for the watch. If someone—a spouse, a girlfriend, a roommate, or somebody close to the killer has accidentally stumbled upon the watch, maybe they would be willing to come forward if we offer financial compensation. After all, money talks," I reasoned.

Williams eyed me thoughtfully for a few minutes. "Okay, I'm definitely willing to explore this idea," he replied. "Let's work out the details and see what happens."

The next week I met with Williams and Rider to hash out the specifics of the reward. During our meeting, Rider said that "while we want people to come forward, we have to remember that a reward offer will stir up people who may be scared, or those who have simply wanted to stay out of the limelight. We need to be sensitive to those who may be genuinely frightened." Rider went on to say, "You also need to prepare yourself for the people who will come forward and give false information in hopes of collecting money. What I guess I am saying, LaDonna, is we need to be prepared for every possible scenario when we launch this reward. This won't be a quick process so pack your patience!"

It turns out that Rider, the man who jokes about being my "murder mentor," was correct. The process of putting the reward together was slow and tedious. The wording of the reward offer was critical. In order to achieve our goal of eliciting new information to move the investigation forward, we had to also ensure that the reward terms were both legal and practical. It took several weeks of back and forth with our attorney, an insurance company, and the police department to finalize things. Once the hard work was completed, we released the following statement:

> Our team is offering a $1,000 CASH REWARD for any information about the Mickey Mouse watch that was worn by Melissa Witt on the evening of December 1, 1994. Any information provided that leads to an arrest and conviction in the abduction and murder of Melissa Witt will receive the $1,000 payout. The community is encouraged to email tips and information to whokilledmissywitt@gmail.com, or to call our anonymous toll-free hotline at: 1-800-440-1922 and leave a detailed message. All informants will be kept confidential.

The reward information was distributed to the media via press release and to the general public through social media platforms including Facebook, Instagram, and Twitter. Days went by. And then weeks. Nothing happened. There seemed to be no interest in the reward. But just as I was starting to lose hope, I received the following voicemail: "Hi, LaDonna. My name is Janie Jones. I am a true crime writer for AY Magazine. Would you be willing to give me an interview for my column? I would like to write a series about the Melissa Witt murder investigation. I am especially interested in the Mickey Mouse watch angle. Could you give me a call back?"

I was ecstatic that she wanted to interview me. I called her back immediately. Jones, an Arkansas native, has spent the last few decades writing feature articles for local publications, but her most notable work was near and dear to my heart—murder mysteries. Jones and I set up a time to talk the following week to discuss the Witt case in detail.

The next week, as scheduled, Jones called my cell phone. She introduced herself and then said, "I'm so excited to talk to you about the Melissa Witt case. The work you have completed on this case to date is remarkable! I, too, want to see justice prevail!" It was refreshing to talk with someone who was truly interested in Melissa's case and was focused on the same goal: justice. During our call, Jones' interest was piqued when I told her about another murder victim—Melissa Trotter. Trotter, if you recall, was a 19-year-old college student from Conroe, Texas who was kidnapped and strangled in circumstances very similar to Melissa Witt's. Like Melissa Witt, Trotter's body was found in a national forest—50 miles away from the abduction site. Remarkably, Trotter was also wearing a Mickey Mouse watch. Trotter's watch, like Witt's, has never been recovered. The man convicted of Trotter's murder, Larry Swearingen, is also the number one suspect in the murder of Melissa Witt.

"There are just too many coincidences in these cases," Jones said. "I can't wait to tell this story. I hope it makes a difference."

The next month, AY Magazine released the first of a two-part series written by Janie Jones entitled, "Murder Mystery. The Mickey Mouse Killer." Jones did a fantastic job in weaving together the complicated twists and turns of the Witt and Trotter cases to tell a compelling story.

After the magazine article was released, I emailed my documentary team, along with Detectives Rider and Williams. "Let's raise the reward amount," I wrote. "Now is the perfect time to do it. I think it's possible that someone has seen Melissa's Mickey Mouse watch, so let's raise the stakes." The team agreed to the idea, and within two weeks, the new reward amount was released: "$5,000 for Information Leading to the Recovery of Melissa Witt's Mickey Mouse Watch."

"This will get someone's attention," I thought. "$5,000 is just too much money to ignore."

It turns out, I was right. The next day, I received the following Facebook message: "I need to talk to someone about a Mickey Mouse watch I found near Sugar Loaf Lake in the summer of 1995. I still have the watch, and I think maybe I should turn it in to authorities in the Witt case. Could you come and pick this watch up and give it to the police?"

I snapped a screenshot of the Facebook message and sent it over to Detective Williams. "This is an interesting tip. I know that Witt frequently spent time with her friends in the Sugar Loaf Lake area," I wrote. "If this is Melissa's watch, I wonder how it ended up there."

Instead of writing back, Williams called. "Do not pick up that watch," he instructed. "It's critical that we preserve the chain of evidence," he said. The chain of evidence, I had learned, is a series of events which, when viewed in sequence, account for the actions of a person during a particular period of time or the location of a piece of evidence during a specified time period. "If this is Melissa's watch," said Williams, "we need to be incredibly careful that we follow the correct process and procedures."

"Absolutely," I agreed. "I completely understand." I provided Detective Williams with the contact information he needed and said, "I hope this tip pans out. Fingers crossed!"

A few hours later, my phone alerted me to a new text message: "I have the watch. Rider and I will call you as soon as we know something," Williams wrote. Finally, at 8:00pm, my phone rang. "Well?" I answered. "The suspense is killing me."

Rider hesitated and then said, "It's not Melissa's watch."

I let out a long sigh. "Damn. How disappointing."

"Don't be disappointed. The reward is working. There is forward movement in the case," Rider assured me. "We just have to stay the course."

Over the next few months, the reward offer brought in dozens of calls and emails of alleged Mickey Mouse watch sightings. As predicted, many of the calls were fake, but others were credible enough to warrant further investigation. The end result, however, was the same: Melissa's Mickey Mouse watch was nowhere to be found. Despite my growing frustration, I continued to heed Rider's advice to "stay the course" by continuing to promote the information as often as possible.

Several months after launching the $5,000 reward, I took the day off to spend some time with my five youngest children. After a day of shoe shopping, ice cream, and fun, we stopped at the grocery store on the way home. The smallest two children rode inside the cart, while the three older ones walked beside me through the store. I distinctly recall standing on the cereal aisle when Paige pointed and said, "Mom, that man is following us." As I looked in his direction, the man slipped around the corner at the end of the aisle. "Stay close to me," I insisted. "Let's walk to the other end of the store and we will finish our shopping."

Ten minutes later, Paige grabbed my arm. "Mom, there he is again!"

"Paige, he's probably just shopping like we are," I assured her.

"But he doesn't have a cart or any groceries," my other daughter, Kennedy, reasoned.

I stood at the end of the laundry detergent aisle and made eye contact with the strange man. He tore his eyes from my gaze and immediately retreated in the other direction.

I turned my cart around to head back across the store. "Mom!" Kennedy pointed. "He's following us." Kennedy was right. There was no denying it. This man was following my children and me through the store.

Alarmed, I reminded all of the kids to stay close to me. "Let's make our way to customer service or a manager," I said calmly. "We're fine," I assured. "He has probably mistaken us for someone he knows."

We had only gone a short distance when the man came out of nowhere and jumped in front of my cart. "I know you," he said. "You are LaDonna Humphrey."

"Who are you?" I demanded. My youngest son, Jaxon, began to cry. "You are scaring my children!"

The man jammed his hands inside the pockets of his tattered jean jacket and looked down at his feet. "You're the lady working on the Melissa Witt case. I know who you are."

"This is neither the time or the place, sir," I replied. "Please move away from my cart and stay away from my family."

As I tried to redirect the cart full of groceries and my five small children to safety, the man blocked our path. "I really need to talk to you, lady," he pleaded. "When I saw you at the ice cream shop, I knew it was you so I followed you here. I want to talk to you."

My jaw dropped. The children and I had left the ice cream shop almost two hours ago. "Get away from my children," I insisted. My voice, loud and panicked, echoed across the store. Another shopper looked my way. "Call the police," I demanded. "Do it now."

The man, unfazed by my reaction, took a step closer. "I want to give you these, lady," he said as he pulled a hand out of one of his dirty pockets. He pushed his open palm in my direction, revealing three dilapidated Mickey Mouse watches. "Take them," he barked.

Stunned, I recoiled at the sight of the watches. "Who are you?" I demanded.

Instead of answering, the man tossed the watches into my cart full of groceries and sprinted across the store. "Someone stop him," I yelled. But it was too late. The stranger disappeared out the door and into the parking lot.

Frightened and confused, I stood motionless in the middle of the grocery store. I was horrified by what had just taken place. My jumbled thoughts were quickly interrupted by the sound of my three-year-old squealing. "Mickey Mouse!" Audrey cheered as she reached inside the cart for the watches.

"Don't touch those sweet girl," I replied. "They do not belong to us."

Audrey began to wail with disappointment as I rushed across the store to the checkout counter. Once there, I used a plastic bag as a makeshift glove to safely secure the watches inside a separate sack. I tied off the bag of watches, placed it carefully in my purse, and paid for my groceries. When my transaction was complete, the store manager walked my family to the safety of our car and assisted me in loading both my children and the groceries into my Suburban. My hands shook as I gripped the steering wheel. I backed out of my parking spot and immediately drove to the police station. Once I arrived in the parking lot, I made two phone calls. One to my husband, and one to Jay C. Rider. Both men were stunned by the series of events that had unfolded.

An investigation ensued, but our efforts to identify the peculiar man from the grocery store were unsuccessful. We were able to determine, however, that none of the Mickey Mouse watches were related to Melissa Witt's murder.

After the frightening events at the grocery store, it was necessary to take measures to ensure the safety of my family, but I did not allow the incident to derail my efforts. Instead, I pushed the fear I felt aside, and continued to promote the $5,000 reward offer through media interviews and social media posts.

Regardless of our relentless passion and drive, it's still been a challenge for my team to agree on a definition of success with the Mickey Mouse watch campaign. Are we successful only if we find Melissa's watch? Or is success found in the number of people that come forward to report information? The measure of success in these efforts, it seems, is inherently subjective. Jay C. Rider, however, believes our team has achieved multiple levels of victory in Melissa's case. "The investigation is revived… but not just revived, it's now on steroids. Before you came along, there was little information on the Internet about the Witt case. Now, a simple Google search pulls up dozens of stories about Melissa's murder," Rider said enthusiastically one afternoon. "People stop me everywhere I go and ask me about her case and they ask me about that Mickey Mouse watch. The public has taken notice, LaDonna. A break in the case is bound to happen because of these efforts. I'm convinced of it. That, my friend, is success."

Successful or not, I've stayed true to our mission and I have continued to do everything in my power to locate Melissa's Mickey Mouse watch. I've fielded dozens of calls, emails, and Facebook messages in response to the $5,000 reward. Those tips have resulted in everything from multiple police interrogations to a house raid. The most recent development, however, surfaced as I put my fingers to the keyboard one afternoon, pouring my heart and soul into the final chapters of this book. My cell phone rang and I reluctantly took a break to answer the unknown caller. "LaDonna Humphrey, how can I help you?" I answered.

A vaguely familiar voice greeted me with, "LaDonna, you may not remember me, but I met you last year… you interviewed me in the Witt case."

The caller then identified himself and the pieces started to come together.

"Oh yes, of course. I remember you," I assured him. The tone of his voice prompted me to ask, "Is everything okay?"

"I have something strange to report. I wanted to contact you right away," his voice cracked under the weight of the news he carried.

"Sure, okay. What's going on?" I replied gently.

"A buddy of mine," he said, his voice just above a whisper, "has a friend that found something important in an abandoned house last week. LaDonna, I think it's really important."

"What did your friend find?" I asked.

"He found a box, LaDonna. A box full of old, vintage, women's Mickey Mouse watches. I can send you a picture of the box of watches if you want," he offered.

"Please do," I stated firmly. "But I also need the name and phone number of the person who has the box. It has to be turned over to the police immediately. Please text me the information. And thank you for calling me. You're right. This is incredibly important."

I hung up the phone and waited for his text. Seconds later, I jumped out of my seat when an image of multiple Mickey Mouse watches showed up in my inbox. "Oh my goodness," I said out loud. I forwarded the screenshot to Detective Marion and to Jay C. Rider with the message: "These watches were found in an abandoned house in the River Valley within the last week. Could one of these watches belong to Witt?" Within minutes, Rider was calling. "Notify Marion right away," he instructed.

"Already did," I replied.

My phone beeped, alerting me to an incoming call.

"I have to go, Marion is on the other line," I said matter-of-factly before disconnecting our call.

"Give me the details," said Detective Marion. As requested, I walked him through the information provided by the informant.

"I'm on it," he promised. "Oh, one more thing. After this call, please email me a report with all of this information. I will be in touch soon."

My heart was racing as I emailed him my report. As soon as I hit send, my phone rang again. It was Rider.

"Marion's on his way to get the watches," I answered.

"Good," said Rider. "This lead has big potential."

"What happens next?" I asked.

"Same as always," Rider chuckled. "Now we wait. Tick-Tock."

Chapter Twenty
A LETTER TO MELISSA'S KILLER

When this journey began in 2015, my team and I had only one goal—to complete a documentary about the abduction and murder of Melissa Witt. Our plan was to share Melissa's story with the world in hopes of seeing her case resolved. Looking back, it's clear that we were all naive in our belief that this project would be completed in 6-8 months with little to no impact on our personal lives. I'm actually quoted in an interview as saying, "We're excited to tackle this project. Our plan is to complete this documentary in less than a year and quickly move on to our next project." At the time I had no idea that the murder of a 19-year-old college student would forever alter the course of my life.

Over the past seven years, I have frequently been asked the same question: Do you have any regrets about the amount of time and energy you have spent working on the Witt case? Without hesitation, my response is always the same: "I have absolutely no regrets." And while I didn't initially set out to devote my life to solving Melissa's murder, fate had other plans. Fighting for justice on her behalf has become a large portion of my life's work. In fact, just yesterday a reporter asked me, "Do you think Melissa's killer is concerned that your life's work is fueled by the passion to see this case solved?" My response: "I sure as hell hope he is. He needs to be… because I won't give up. Ever."

The man that murdered Melissa Witt created irreparable damage for her family, her friends, and an entire community. The suffering that was borne from Melissa's death demands justice. And the only way to achieve that goal is to aggressively seek out the last few pieces of the intricate puzzle surrounding her murder. When those pieces are found and put in place, the world will finally know once and for all who killed Melissa Witt.

As fate would have it, I am standing on the very cusp of the 27th anniversary of Melissa's murder as I write this final chapter. It seems only fitting that the closing words I pen are meant for only one person—Melissa's murderer:

> I continue an exhaustive search for you. Even on the days when the sun is shining and I walk down the street with my family, I am searching. Until I find you, I will forever gaze into every crowd and wonder if you are there among the sea of faces.
> Are you a dark and dreadful serial killer spending your life methodically

killing innocent young women? Or a coward hiding behind the cloak of mundane normalcy? Either way, you are a man that carries evil in his heart—a curse that permeates every ounce of your being.

I see you—a sad, pathetic womanizer whose life is filled with broken relationships, chaos, anger issues, impotence, and fear. This is who you are—a man whose fragile ego demanded he murder a beautiful 19-year-old girl.

How often do you relive that December night when Melissa rejected your advances—the moment you felt so humiliated, angry, and small? When I close my eyes, I can envision the moment Melissa refused to acquiesce to your selfish demands. I want to scream and warn her to run. But it's too late. I watch as your white hot rage swells. I open my eyes. I know what comes next. My heart will not allow me to imagine it.

Your thoughts, I know, were clouded by visions of murder as you drove deep into the Ozark National Forest that cold December night. The only witnesses to your crime were the white oak trees and shortleaf pine that trembled and swayed as Melissa's terrified screams echoed through their leaves and into the dark abyss of the forest.

Decades later, as I stood underneath the same tall shadowed trees and among the clumps of bushes and snaking undergrowth that once embraced the lifeless body of Melissa Witt, I vowed to find you. And I will.

But until that day arrives, our lives will remain intertwined—connected by fate—through the common thread of a girl you brutally murdered—a girl I never knew.

EPILOGUE

"Dear Ms. Humphrey,

I apologize for contacting you through your private email account. I wanted to reach out to you because the person who gave me this email said that you were working on a documentary about the Melissa Witt murder but they also suggested you were looking into the death fetish community. Please allow me to share some information that I think might be of interest to you and also your investigation.

I grew up in Greenwood, Arkansas and we moved to Memphis in 1995. I finished high school there. I don't remember many details about Melissa Witt's murder, just the name. I should ask my wife about these things. She listens to Serial and several other true crime shows. She's also into all these books too. It's funny. When I told her about my silly interest in girls playing dead she didn't even bat an eye! Forgive me for being blunt. I hope I'm not scaring you, Ms. Humphrey. I would never want to do that.

Anyway, I would like to tell you about someone named Jessica. You see, she finds a lot of sites in the fantasy community but also in the real life snuff community. She gets off on real death. Real crime scene and autopsy stuff. That's way beyond fantasy. My friend Bill, who works with a producer, confirmed a few days ago that Jessica paid off two girls who were sexually abused by a producer. He even provided the dates and amounts of these payments to me via email.

What I'm trying to say is, you can make a connection here. There is definitely bad stuff happening. I'm no journalist (writing never was my jam) but it seems to me you've got an easy narrative: The tragic death of a young girl and a community that exists today that gets off on things like that. You do know about the death fetish community, right? Someone told me you have been poking your nose around places that you don't belong. You should be afraid of these people who write about women being strangled and raped, their bodies violated, and more. They glorify it. In fact, you should be utterly terrified.

I do hope you won't play coy, Ms. Humphrey. I think you could be onto something big here. I am a little afraid for you, though. And for your friend. You know, the one that is helping you investigate all of this? It's very dangerous.

But you do seem brave, Ms. Humphrey. So if you have some time, look up a man named Joe Schwalenberg. What happened to him was a big deal. He was a part of an old death fantasy site, and one of its members killed someone in real life. He claimed the death fantasy community that encouraged violence against women made him feel accepted and understood. There are some incredibly dangerous people in the death fantasy/fetish world, Ms. Humphrey. I hope you are taking this seriously. Real people are getting killed.

So surely, you can easily see the connection I am trying to make. Melissa died before this online community existed, but clearly there's a story here of men being shown that violence is okay. Men who fantasize about murdering women in the same fashion in which Melissa Witt was killed. Surely, Ms. Humphrey, you can see the connection too. Right? Melissa's killer could roam among them. Are you afraid? I really think you should be.

Men and women in these online communities are committing real crimes. No one listens to me. They block or ban me. I hoped maybe you'd take what I have to say seriously. I need someone to listen, Ms. Humphrey. Someone brave. Someone like you.

Before I go, I want to tell you this: I think the person who killed Melissa Witt was someone looking for the sexual thrill of dominating and killing a young woman. Often though, the gender of the victim doesn't even matter quite as much. Any sexual thrill a sadistic person like this gets is likely from the act of dominating and killing, it is not based on what gender they happen to be. But anyone can have preferences, it's true. I suspect that it was someone that knew Melissa Witt far more than she knew them. Someone who appeared kind and, most importantly, unassuming. The nature of the crime would rule out it being a crime of passion or opportunity, mainly because this person appears to have thought this all through. Perhaps they knew her well enough to get her to trust them in a moment of need (a car ride, for example) or something to that effect, and that's when they killed her.

This type of person would likely be someone that had a desire to hurt and kill from a very young age. They probably would be the type to think about these things a lot, read comics and books that featured a pretty intense level of violence, and who might have written stories for themselves or did other creative things to get their fantasies out. Usually these things start out as a fantasy, and as the person gets older these fantasies start to take on a sexual leaning. They want more and yearn for more. Their fantasies get more and more intense until the fantasy aspect is no longer appealing and they want the real thing. And then… boom! They kill someone like the beautiful, young Melissa Witt.

But here's the most important question to ask yourself as you seek justice for Melissa Witt. And you do want justice, don't you Ms. Humphrey? If so, I think you have to ask yourself these questions: Was this his first effort at taking a life or was this part of a longer series of murders? Just how far are you willing to go to find out the truth? Will fear paralyze you? Or will you charge on towards justice, despite the terrifying realities of what you may face? Whatever will you do, Ms. Humphrey? I almost can't wait to find out.

Have a nice evening. And please, whatever you do, try to stay safe.

The Vermillion Strangler"

ACKNOWLEDGMENTS

My amazing husband, Danny Humphrey—Thank you for all of the late night editing sessions, endless amounts of patience, sound advice, amazing encouragement, and constant supply of Diet Coke. I simply could not have done this without you, my love. My heart is yours, forever.

My littlest loves, Paige, Kennedy, Jaxon, Audrey, and Isabella—Somehow, despite all of the constant interruptions, chaos, and giggles, I managed to write this book! Thank you for always cheering me on!

My dearest Alexandria—Thank you for being my closest confidant, a brutally honest editor, and my constant companion on this journey. I pray this book is all you dreamed it could be and more. Thank you for believing in me. I love you more than you can ever comprehend.

My son, Nik—Thank you for always believing in me. Your love and support gave me the confidence to chase this dream. I love and admire you, son.

Misty—There are not enough words to describe what you mean to me. Thank you for standing by me and cheering me on!

Amy—Where do I begin? There is so much to say, but I think maybe I can sum it up best in three little letters: NWH!

Jay C. Rider—You are so much more than a mentor – you are also one of my most cherished friends. Thank you for your willingness to teach this rookie everything you know. Marlena Yarberro—Thank you for putting up with all of our endless late night phone calls and for being a constant source of friendship, love, and support. This book would not be possible without either of you. You both have my respect, gratitude, love, and friendship— forever.

Nic Edwards, Chris Boyd, and Joshua Kessler— Thank you for embracing and encouraging my quest for justice in Melissa's case. I am humbled by your support and honored to call you each my friend.

Alecia Lockhart—This journey has brought me many things, but your friendship is by far the most memorable and valuable gift. There is no stopping us!

Leya Booth—Thank you for believing in this project from day one. The journey to bring this book to life has been incredible! I am so grateful for your friendship, encouragement, stellar editing skills, and the confidence you have given me to believe in myself. Thank you, friend.

Kristina Young—My heart is broken that you did not live to see this book come to fruition. Every word written in this book was fueled by the love and support that you so graciously poured into my life for so many years. You will never be forgotten—sisters for life!

Levi Risley, Troy Williams, Brad Marion, Aric Mitchell, Rebecca Duke, James Renner, Angie Baker, Daren Bob, Jo Ellison, Jacob Cotner, Connor Holmes, Tara Limbird, Sarah Butcher, Janie Jones, Marla Cantrell, Allen Woody, Kurtis Sutley, Leslie Reinhart, Marcus Blair, Anita Dodson, Melanie Neal, Janna Hines, Lauren Mincy, Sharon Camp, Amber Gassman, Nathan Oliver, Tom Stockland, Jera Houghtaling, Kelley Humphrey, Jordan Stramiello, Thomas Landrum, Lesa Crowell, Sarah Livengood, Lauren McLemore, Marc Hoover, Melissa Ann Morgan Humphreys, True Crime Garage, United States of Murder, Catch My Killer Podcast, Abnormal Arkansas, Crimepedia Podcast, Serial Writers Production, KUAF, The Murder History Girls Podcast, Just the Tip-sters Podcast, Southwest Times Record, KFSM News, Fort Smith Police Department, Genius Book Publishing, and AY Magazine—thank you for believing in **#justiceformelissawitt**.

Made in United States
Orlando, FL
20 March 2023

31226022R00134